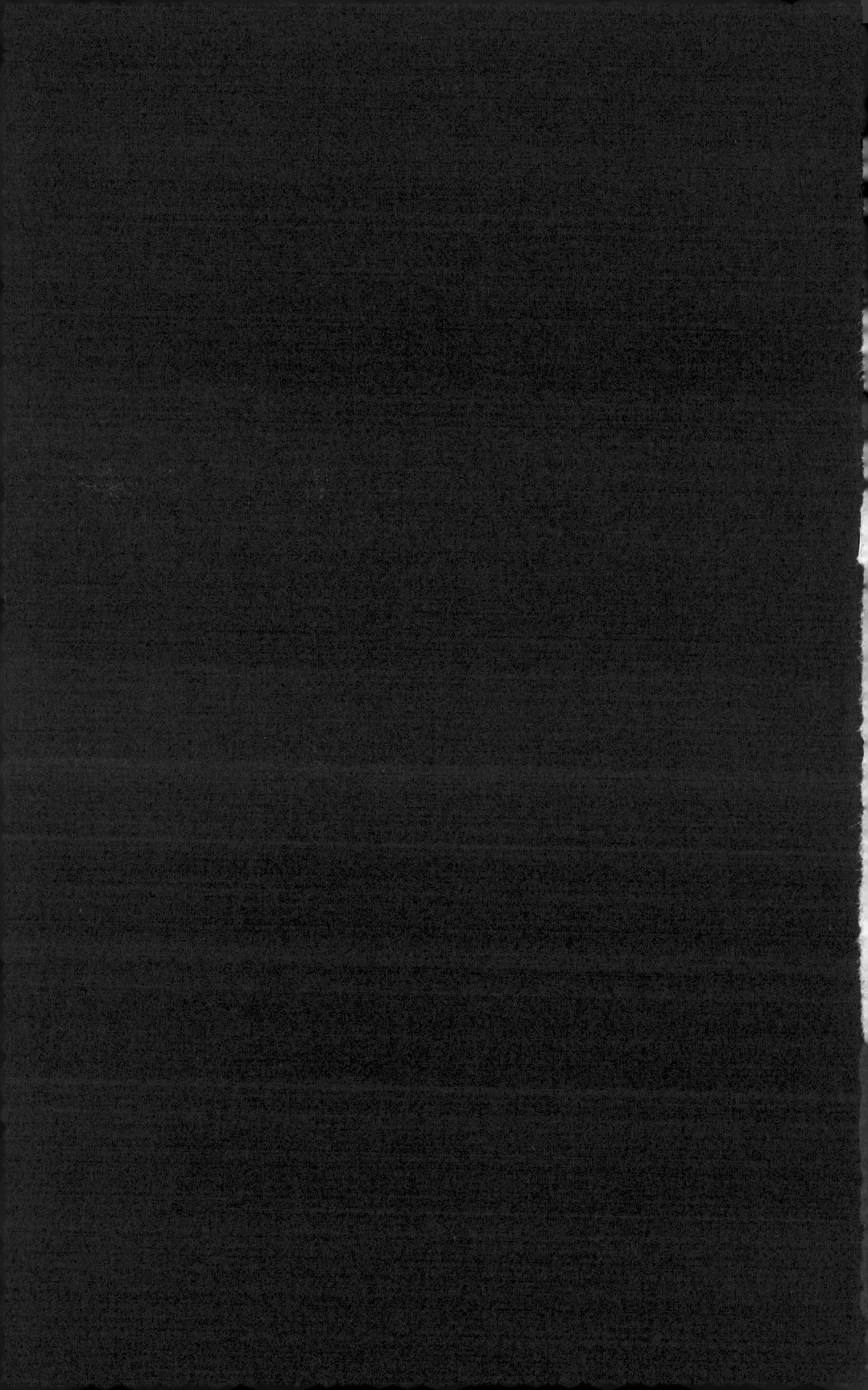

The Comical as

Textual Practice in

Les Fleurs du Mal

John W. MacInnes

The Comical as Textual Practice in Les Fleurs du Mal

University Presses of Florida

University of Florida Press/Gainesville

Library of Congress Cataloging in Publication Data

MacInnes, John W., 1946–
    The comical as textual practice in *Les fleurs du mal.*

    Bibliography: p.
    Includes index.
    1. Baudelaire, Charles, 1821–1867. Fleurs du mal.
    2. Baudelaire, Charles, 1821–1867—Humor, satire, etc.
    3. Comic, The, in literature.   I. Title.
    PQ2191.F63M24   1988   841'.8   87–14269
    ISBN 0-8130-0866-2

UNIVERSITY PRESSES OF FLORIDA is the central agency for scholarly publishing of the State of Florida's university system, producing books selected for publication by the faculty editorial committees of Florida's nine public universities: Florida A&M University (Tallahassee), Florida Atlantic University (Boca Raton), Florida International University (Miami), Florida State University (Tallahassee), University of Central Florida (Orlando), University of Florida (Gainesville), University of North Florida (Jacksonville), University of South Florida (Tampa), University of West Florida (Pensacola).

ORDERS for books published by all member presses should be addressed to University Presses of Florida, 15 NW 15th Street, Gainesville, FL 32603.

Part of chapter 2 in this volume appeared as an article in *French Forum* (January 1987) and is reproduced here with the permission of the publisher.

To Jane and Patricia MacInnes

good friends both

Contents

Preface

In recent years, French thinking at the intersection of philosophy, literature, and psychoanalysis has buttressed in this country a number of welcome new strategies of reading. It is not surprising that a powerful, and at times polemical, rereading of Baudelaire has resulted from our concern with the writings of Lacan, Kristeva, Derrida, de Man, *et al.* It is perhaps less surprising for scholars working on Baudelaire than for others, since this recent inquiry has enabled readers of Baudelaire to continue a mode of inquiry that was first opened by Walter Benjamin before the Second World War. In a work that remained unfinished at the time of his death, Benjamin had combined a materialist methodology, a familiarity with psychoanalytic theory, and a gifted sensibility to arrive at insights that have yet to be fully explored, concerning Baudelaire's texts.[1] In their rearticulation of his inquiry, contemporary critics have, like Benjamin, situated Baudelaire in the midst of a cultural and historical crisis; also like him, they regard the poet as acutely alive to the ramifications of that crisis regarding the role of the poet and of poetry in the modern world; and they share with Benjamin a tactic whereby current psychoanalytic theory is brought to bear upon a text, not in order to delineate an author's psychological motivation, but rather in order to show how writing suggests limitations, blind spots, and determinations of consciousness. Let me begin, then, by situating briefly my own inquiry in relation to two major essays that deal with Baudelaire by rearticulating the Benjaminian problematic.

Leo Bersani's *Baudelaire and Freud* opens with the following statement:

> Baudelaire's work can be viewed as an exemplary drama in our culture. It illustrates in striking fashion both the persistence and the subversion of idealistic vision in modern literature. Baudelaire continuously returns to categories discredited by the experiences evoked in his most original writing . . . . The two "postulations"—as well as the entire moral and religious vocabulary to which they give rise in Baudelaire—can in fact be thought of as an escape from the anxieties produced by the Baudelairean discovery of psychic mobility, or unanchored identity.[2]

For Bersani, Baudelaire and Freud both lived through a "critical moment in our cultural history," and both expressed as well as repressed in their writing the unsettling insights revealed in the course of that cultural drama. Relying heavily on Lacan's distinction between Imaginary and Symbolic modes of self-apprehension, Bersani finds Baudelaire's writing split between the fixity of the Imaginary and the "mobility" of the Symbolic. In the Symbolic order, the self comes to renounce its quest for a hypostatized identity perceived in a specular and mirroring relation to an exterior presence. It accepts, instead, that the self is in essence mobile, and that the desire that propels it toward the future is, in fact, modeled upon an irrecuperable past. The self of the Symbolic order is open to what Bersani calls "the creative mobility of fantasy": this is the self that Baudelaire dramatizes in his erotic scenes. When not overcome by fantasies of erotic desire, the poet reverts, however, to the idealistic image of the self as a fixed and contained site of integrity. In this, the Imaginary mode of self-representation, the poet writes out his tendency to seek his image in the world about him. In the Imaginary mode, the self seeks to capture itself in reflections of identity-in-the-other—or in "allegories" of selfhood.

Bersani thus splits Baudelaire's work into two unequal and mutually exclusive parts. On the one hand, we have the love poems, which reveal an "original" sense of the self through the discovery of the extent to which the identity of both the desiring subject and the desired object can be lost amid a sea of fantasy associations. On the other hand, we have the defensive stance of this transitional poet, in which the recourse to allegory will serve as the means of stabilizing the self by establishing a stable and specular "meaning" in the world. The poet's work of interpreting the world is discredited as no more than the desire of the self to fixate itself in the meaningful stability of its interpretations. In Bersani's optic, we see Baudelaire working under the shadow of anxiety—not the "anxiety of influence" proposed by Harold Bloom, but rather the anxiety of "psychic mobility, of unanchored identity" that Bersani equates with castration anxiety.

For Bersani, anxiety does not reside in the poet's wish to differentiate himself from his predecessors, but rather in his wish to maintain the claim to a unified and unifying agency of selfhood, exercised as the attempt to immobilize meaning. Recent French inter-pretations of psychoanalytic theory point toward "a formulation of the castration complex in terms of *an anguished preoccupation with the mobility of meaning*" (Bersani's emphasis, 59). Baudelaire, he argues, resides under the sign of that anxious preoccupation. The poet emerges as a kind of fetishist who occasionally finds himself writing out a radical new image of the self in poems where both subjectivity and textuality resist coherency and closure, but who denies that radical image in most of his work, preferring the enclosure of self and text through allegorical totalization. Allegory becomes the im-mobilizing response to the anxiety over whether self-sense and po-etic sense can reflect each other in stable containment. Allegory, in Bersani's reading, is the trope of the Imaginary order. Fragmenta-tion becomes a phenomenon that is as threatening as it is erotically fascinating; against this phenomenon an ill-tempered and repressive poet mobilizes the stabilizing power of allegory. "The allegorization of desire," says Bersani, "as Baudelaire himself illustrates, is a major sign of both a cultural and an individual repression of desire as per-manently displaced" (62).

In a sense, Bersani's work continues Benjamin's, since it employs contemporary psychoanalytical insights to explicate texts that issue from a period of historical crisis. But where Benjamin's essays result in a complex and contradictory Baudelaire who, like Walt Whitman, contains multitudes, Bersani's argument for the mobility of selves ends up by fixing Baudelaire between the poles of a single set of oppositions, organized around Lacan's distinction between the Imaginary and the Symbolic orders. One can certainly take excep-tion to Bersani's argument that the fluid figurality of the love poems can be equated with an escape from self-consciousness.[3] I wish for the moment only to point out the contradiction in an argument for "mobility" that so restricts the self of its primary object. To fix Baudelaire's writing at either of two poles, valorizing the one and decrying the rigidity of the other, amounts to a reading of him that owes a great deal to the specular play of the Imaginary order. It is difficult to see how the dangers of imaginary thinking can be avoided in an act of repetition. In the pages that follow, I will pay close attention to Baudelaire's allegorical poems, hoping to compli-cate somewhat Bersani's interpretation of allegory as the index of narcissistic specularity, anxiously deployed against the mobility of sense.

The second major work to continue Benjamin's path of investigation is Barbara Johnson's *Défigurations du langage poétique: la seconde révolution baudelairienne.*[4] This intricately argued book could well have as its epigraph one of Benjamin's concluding remarks from "On Some Motifs in Baudelaire": "And, finally, it cannot be denied that some of his motifs—and the present study has dealt with them—render the possibility of lyric poetry questionable." For Johnson, it is not Baudelaire's motifs, but rather the strategic rhetoric of his prose poems, that serves to call into question the status of the lyrical in modern sensibility. The prose poems do not, in her analysis, undermine the status of certain verse "doublets" merely by showing that there is no guaranteed difference between poetry and prose, but instead by foregrounding the play of difference within all language. The poem-in-prose invites us, Johnson writes,

> à interroger non pas la différence entre poésie et prose, mais la nature d'un besoin de différence à l'intérieur de la langue, besoin qui persiste au-delà de toutes ses manifestations particulières. Les poèmes en prose de Baudelaire et de Mallarmé marquent en effet un moment de crise où la mise en question d'*une* différence devient parole sur *la* différence. (10)

The crisis that is invoked above consists in the turn away from verse, toward a language that reflects upon the self-satisfied pretensions of lyricism. To demonstrate the degree of reflexivity involved in the writing of the prose poems, Johnson reads several of the so-called "doublet" texts—*La Chevelure* and *Un Hémisphère dans une chevelure*, for example—against each other, noting how the prose texts consistently undermine the rhetorical stance of their verse counterparts.

Although Johnson's reading parts ways with Bersani concerning the conclusion to be drawn from the fluid mass of imagery in the love poems, she nonetheless shares with him an interest in pointing out the potentially narcissistic function of a privileged language claiming to be "poetic." For Bersani, that language is typified by allegorization; for Johnson, it is signaled by versification itself. This adoption of the ready-made split between verse texts and prose texts grants her a far greater flexibility in her rhetorical analyses, and allows for readings of specific texts that are exhaustively detailed. But it also leaves intact a heuristic dualism that implicitly accords a privileged value to any and all prose poems over any and all verse texts. Such a founding opposition is perhaps inherent in any critical reading that posits a single crisis as its object of investigation, by virtue of the very nature of the notion of "crisis." Nevertheless, it is a problematic move to align categorically Baudelaire's verse with such suspect qualities as symmetrical dual relations, correspondence, analogy, fusion, proliferation of substitutes, and metaphoric totalization, while championing the prose texts for exercising an opposed rhetoric of eccentric relations, difference, contiguity, separateness, open-ended enumeration, and metonymic addition.

Johnson herself appears troubled by this basic strategy: thoroughgoing reader that she is, she must account for the fact that *La Chevelure* ends by posing a question that might lead some readers to suspect that the poem ultimately challenges—without recourse to the prose "doublet"—its own seductive rhetoric. The poem ends as follows:

> N'es-tu pas l'oasis où je rêve, et la gourde
> Où je hume à long traits le vin du souvenir?[5]

The problem posed by this rhetorical question leads Johnson to ask questions about the question:

> Pourquoi cette apothéose de la métaphoricité, ce changement de l' "être" de la destinatrice, prend-elle la forme d'une question? et plus précisément, d'une question rhétorique? La question rhétorique étant l'exemple par excellence du divorce potentiel entre le signifiant (la forme interrogative) et le signifié (le sens affirmatif), cette formulation équivoque de la métaphore finale ne met-elle pas en question précisément la transparence de la rhétorique métaphorique qu'elle résume? (51)

If the poem's question is not rhetorical, then it questions the validity of the metaphor that it puts forth. If the question is indeed rhetorical, it still undermines the congruency of the metaphorical relation by offering it in a statement whose form and sense assert themselves as different. Johnson admits that this *double impasse* threatens the happy *illusion métaphorique* that she finds at work in the poem; but, since she is committed to an opposition that must relegate the verse texts to a secondary status, she is forced to reduce the power of the poem's final lines as follows:

> Cette interrogation équivoque, qui semble mettre en question les rapports symétriques esquissés par le poème, confine pourtant à une alternance binaire (vraie question/fausse question; (réponse) non/(réponse) oui) qui n'est en réalité qu'une variante du rapport duel, symétrique, qu'elle suspend. Tout en mettant en question la validité de la métaphore, la question rhétorique laisse le *fonctionnement* de la métaphore intact. Or, la question que pose le poème en prose n'est pas: "la métaphore est-elle vraie ou fausse?" mais: "*comment* la métaphore fonctionne-t-elle?" (51–52)

Johnson here answers her own questions, in a way that indicates that even if the rhetorical status of the poem's question is undecidable, the rhetoricity of her questions remains intact. To the question about why the verse poem ends as it does, we are told to answer merely: "Why not, since it makes no difference." But in order for us to answer in that way, we must first accept the proposition that a rhetorical question demands in response *either* a "yes" or a "no"— never a "yes" *and* a "no," and never a response that calls the reader beyond the limits of a binary logic. Such a posture on the part of a critic who displays elsewhere in the book an extraordinary subtlety in analysis and interpretation reflects a certain straining to maintain the categorical opposition that grounds her reading. Because her reading cannot but be grounded in the power of a traditional opposition at the same time that it is founded on the sense that the traditional difference between such categories can be shown to consist more truly in the difference within each one—for reasons derived precisely from the power of her argument—one is led to suspect that the verse poems are themselves worthy of a more patient consideration.

By suggesting that certain verse texts attain a degree of complexity and irreducibility comparable to those of the most intransigent prose texts, I shall, in effect, attenuate the severity of Johnson's unavoidable devaluation of the verse poetry of Baudelaire. My reading, then, wishes no more, and no less, than to question the gesture whereby the work of Baudelaire is understood on the basis of an overriding yet confining dualism, whether that dualism be between the flesh and the spirit, woman and God, the Imaginary and the Symbolic, or the prosaic and the rhymed. I will focus on texts that address the problem of allegory—since that trope most acutely poses the relation between writing and meaning. Baudelaire dealt in that relation for as long as he wrote verse: the very persistence of allegorization in his work might well caution us against positing a crisis that would split his writing into moments of a "before" and an "after." I shall suggest that the crisis that is lived through Baudelaire's poetry is both iterative and indigenous to the project of his writing. It is a crisis lived over and over, each time the poet feels compelled to offer an interpretation of the world while suspecting simultaneously that interpretation is the lure of the *dupe*—the character who the poet, in Baudelaire's view, must never be.

Though I am solely responsible for whatever failings this study might have, I am also indebted to numerous friends and colleagues who have shared their time and thoughts with me over the years. I especially thank Jonathan Culler, Nelly Furman, Richard Klein, Philip Lewis, and Edward Morris of Cornell, Neil Hertz of Johns Hopkins, and François Rigolot of Princeton for their advice. My warm thanks go to Shirley Shultz and Norma Singleton, who not only offered their time to type parts of the manuscript but were always ready to counter my splenetic moments. Finally, I thank Janet Gordon, the high-school teacher who had the courage to insist that I study French seriously.

1

Le Point de Départ

Une poésie voyante

> Moi? C'est une image que je poursuis, rien
> de plus.
> —Gérard de Nerval, *Sylvie*

If we are to begin by considering "Un Voyage à Cythère," it is in order to assess and interpret what we know of the writing and re-writing of that poem. My goal necessitates that we return to the early months of 1852—to the period roughly bounded by the *coup d'état* of Louis Napoleon on December 2, 1851, and by the plebiscite of March, a few months later. The poem first surfaces in French literary history at that time, when Baudelaire sends a copy of it to Gautier for publication. Since the note that accompanies the poem bears no date, it can only be placed sometime in March of 1852. That approximate dating, however, is enough to situate the first public appearance of the text in a moment of considerable interest. During the winter months, Louis Napoleon legitimates the *coup* by extending the term of the presidency, initiates the most severe press controls since the reign of his namesake, and puts his prefects in charge of backing the official candidates in the March elections. The latter win 253 of the 261 seats in the legislature, and the prefects' salaries are doubled soon after. Meanwhile, the country's most acclaimed poet has not yet sought refuge on Jersey, but is in Brussels writing two political pamphlets, *L'Histoire d'un crime* and *Napoléon le Petit*; Hugo is writing these tracts while Marx finishes the *Eighteenth Brumaire*. And Nerval, less acclaimed than Hugo though more recently the focus of discussion among Baudelaire, Champfleury, and the other collaborators at the short-lived journal *La Semaine thé-âtrale*—in which a review of *Le Voyage en Orient* appears in February—passes from one doctor to another, undergoing successive treatments for erysipelas and "une fièvre chaude."[1]

As for Baudelaire, the period is both stressful and productive. The *coup d'état* and its aftermath apparently lead him to a bitter rejection of politics; he writes to Ancelle that he did not vote in the March elections because he could only have voted for himself. "Le 2 décembre m'a physiquement dépolitisé," he archly declares.[2] The letter does not go on to explain the physical sense of his depoliticization, shifting instead to the subject of his impending separation from Jeanne Duval. Further complicating our judgment of his political position at this time, a letter to Poulet-Malassis dated two weeks later reads: "Parmi toutes les personnes que je connais il n'y a que sottise et passion individuelles. Personne ne consent à se mettre au point de vue *providentiel*."[3] Again, Baudelaire does not clarify his remark by hinting at what might be seen from a providential point of view; he does not suggest that Louis Napoleon is the savior of the nation, for instance, nor that the *coup* is a necessary step toward revolution. Given the inconsistency and contradictions that surround his political opinions and actions, either version of the *coup*'s providentiality might be plausible. It is probably more important at this point to note that the political events of the time come upon Baudelaire as he is in the midst of a personal domestic crisis, rather than to decipher on their own a pair of too-brief references. The letter to Ancelle cited above begins: "Ma tête devient littéralement un volcan malade. De grands orages et de grandes aurores." It ends: "Je relis ma letter, et il me semble qu'elle doit avoir *pour vous un air fou*. Il en sera toujours ainsi." Further, the transition between the passage on his failure to vote and the passage on his separation from Jeanne is accompanied by another confession of agitation: "Ne vous étonnez pas du fouillis de ma lettre; je suis chargé d'idées troublantes." The political humiliation of the *coup d'état* and the private humiliation of the violent debacle of his life with Jeanne arrive simultaneously. And if we have little evidence of what he later calls his "fureur au coup d'état," we have ample evidence of his private rage in a long letter to his mother.[4] Of that letter I will cite only a single sentence—a sentence remarkable for the way in which a cadenced control of exposition brittlely compensates its shrill depiction:

> Vivre avec un etre qui ne vous sait aucun gré de vos efforts, qui les contrarie par une maladresse ou une méchanceté permanente, qui ne vous considère que comme son domestique et sa propriété, avec qui il est impossible d'échanger une parole politique ou littéraire, une créature *qui ne veut rien apprendre,* quoique vous lui ayez proposé de lui donner vous-même des leçons, une créature qui ne m'admire pas, et qui ne s'intéresse

même pas à mes études, qui jetterait mes manuscrits au feu si cela lui rapportait plus d'argent que de les laisser publier, qui renvoie mon chat qui était ma seule distraction au logis, et qui introduit des chiens, *parce que* la vue des chiens me fait mal, qui ne sait pas ou ne veut pas comprendre *qu'être très avare, pendant* UN *mois seulement,* me permettrait, grâce à ce repos momentané, de finir un gros livre,—enfin est-ce possible cela, est-ce possible?[5]

The conflation of shame in the face of both the imperious Jeanne and the imperial *prise de pouvoir*—"J'ai des larmes de honte et de rage dans les yeux en t'écrivant ceci," he writes to his mother, while the journal entry ends: "Encore un Bonaparte! quelle honte!"—is doubtless fueled by Baudelaire's complete lack of funds. We find him writing to the Société des Gens de Lettres for an advance of eighty-five francs!

Nevertheless, the first months of 1852 are a period of considerable productivity. In January *La Semaine théâtrale,* which published *Les Drames et les romans honnêtes* two months earlier, is the site of another critical attack, "L'Ecole païenne." The next month, the now foundering journal publishes a pair of poems, "Les Deux Crépuscules." In March and April, the first long essay on Poe, "Edgar Allan Poe, sa vie et ses ouvrages" appears in *La Revue de Paris.* In the course of the year, several translations of Poe will also be published.

At the age of thirty, however, Baudelaire remains virtually unknown as a writer of verse. A handful of poems appeared the year before, in the *Messager de l'assemblée,* but at least one of Baudelaire's old friends, Ernest Prarond, fears at this time that his gifted colleague may have abandoned all ambition to write poetry.[6] Prarond is mistaken, for Baudelaire has put together a dozen poems to send to Gautier at the *Revue de Paris.* They are sent off in two "paquets," as Baudelaire calls them, in the month of March. Along with the poems in the second package—among them one entitled "Voyage à Cythère"—Gautier finds a note that reads:

L'Incorrigible Gérard prétend au contraire que c'est pour avoir abandonné le bon culte que Cythère est réduite en cet état.

Voilà donc cher ami, ce *second* petit paquet. J'espère que tu trouveras de quoi choisir. Je désire vivement que ton goût s'accorde avec le mien. Pour mon compte, voilà ce que je préfère:

Les deux Crépuscles,
La Caravane,
Le reniement de St Pierre,
L'Artiste inconnu,
L'Outre de la volupté,
La fontaine de Sang,
Le voyage à Cythère.

Protège-moi ferme. Si on ne grogne pas trop contre cette poésie, j'en donnerai de plus *voyante* encore.
    Adieu.

Charles Baudelaire.[7]

Despite Baudelaire's wishes, the harmony of taste among the men involved does not materialize: of the twelve poems sent in March, the progressive-minded journal sees fit to publish only the "Reniement de Saint-Pierre" in its pages. It is at this time that Gautier is said to have predicted: "Baudelaire will misfire as Pétrus Borel did."[8]

I have cited Baudelaire's note to Gautier in full because it makes clear that, despite the possibly obsequious list of favorite poems it contains, it is dominated by concern for one text among the twelve. The opening remark certainly concerns the decline of Cythera-Cerigo, about which Nerval had written in his travelogue articles in 1844, and again in his *Voyage en Orient.* And there is no reason not to hypothesize that the concluding remark about a *poésie voyante,* in so short a note, might also be occasioned by thoughts of the "Voyage à Cythère." We can only "test" that hypothesis by reading the poem in the light of the remark, and vice versa. But before doing so, let me make clear what can, and cannot, be claimed about the early months of 1852 with regard to the text we are about to read. There is no decisive evidence to lead us to conclude that the poem was first written at this time: a liminal note on the manuscript refers to Nerval's articles of 1844 in *L'Artiste;* those articles had been summarized and discussed by Champfleury in an article in 1849, which could be the means of Baudelaire's contact with them; they had also been revised in the *Voyage en Orient,* but there is no reason to believe that Baudelaire was not familiar with them before 1851; we do know, however, that the publication of the *Voyage en Orient* led to an article by Champfleury in *La Semaine théâtrale* in February, and we can assume that the motif of Cythera-Cerigo was at least once more a topic of conversation among Baudelaire, Champfleury, and perhaps Nerval.[9] We cannot assume that the poem was *conceived* at this time, and any desire to do so is thwarted by Baudelaire's often repeated claim that all his poetry is a product of his late adolescence.[10] We are thus led to read the text as a version, to be compared with a later version, but as a version for which there is no master text. The 1857 poem titled "Un Voyage à Cythère" is an active revision of the poem sent to Gautier, as we shall see; but that earlier text can only be regarded as a possible revision of a lost poem written as early as 1844, or as late as 1852. Whatever the case may be, this version of the poem was sent to Gautier out of the biographical and historical situations outlined above, although its true addressee seems to be "*l'incorrigible*" Gérard de Nerval.

Oceanic Feelings

> Le mot *dégoût (Ekel)* ne désigne pas le
> répugnant ou le négatif en général. Il s'agit
> bien de ce qui donne *envie de vomir.*
> Comment avoir *envie* de vomir?
> —Jacques Derrida, *Economimésis*

I will begin by assuming that the application of the epithet "incorrigible" to Nerval implies a certain conscious intent to rectify, and that such an attempt has produced a text that might belong to a poetic class labeled "voyante." This second assumption, however, is not a strong methodological tool, since a *poésie voyante* can as well be a gaudy, startling, garish poetry—a poetic form of yellow journalism—as the second-sighted, all-seeing, or clairvoyant poetry that we have come to identify with the project of Rimbaud. The adjective *voyant,* unlike its nominal derivative, contains both the active and passive senses of visibility and vision, of the seen and the seeing.

Thus the labeling of a poetry as "voyante" might do little more than initiate a curiosity regarding the mode of vision that such a poetry employs, or regarding the deployment of the spectacular in its persuasive strategy, or both.[11] My initial assumption—that Baudelaire produced this text with the conscious intention of setting Nerval straight—is so well founded as merely to repeat the procedure of every scholarly reader. Let us turn briefly to the text that incited Baudelaire to rectification.

The Cerigo episode in the *Voyage en Orient* comprises several chapters of the "Introduction: Vers l'Orient." In chapter 11, Nerval describes crossing the Adriatic in terrible weather, with conditions so bad that most of the passengers are unable to dine and must remain in their hammocks. The description of life on board ship in stormy weather is immediately preceded by the revelation of Nerval's personal motive for undertaking his crossing at the least favorable time of year: "Il faut que j'aie mis l'étendu des mers entre moi et . . . un doux et triste souvenir."[12] The memory that the traveler cannot bring himself to specify is the death of Jenny Colon, the pivotal beloved figure in Nerval's youth, who died in the summer of 1842. Just before Christmas the same year, Nerval had left Paris to begin his journey to the East. The crossing thus takes place in January of the next year. The weather having incommoded most of the passengers, only Nerval and three others remain at table: "Ce qui n'était pour tous qu'un repas devient pour ceux qui restent un festin, qu'on prolonge le plus possible . . . . Il y avait, outre Soliman et moi, un capitaine anglais et un capucin de la terre sainte, nommé le père Charles" (62). One by one, the revelers slowly fade, until only the Englishman is left to down a bottle of champagne. With surprising bravado, he announces that he will finish it alone, and will enjoy a second bottle after that one. He is discovered the next morning, still at table, dead. The narrator comments:

> Etrange destinée! cet Anglais était un ancien capitaine de la compagnie des Indes, souffrant d'une maladie de coeur, et à qui l'on avait conseillé l'eau du Nil. Le vin ne lui a pas donné le temps d'arriver à l'eau.
> Après tout, est-ce là un genre de mort bien malheureux?
> On va s'arrêter à Cérigo pour y laisser le corps de l'Anglais.

> C'est ce qui me permet de visiter cette île, où le bateau ne re-
> lâche pas ordinairement. (63)

Thus it is only the unexpected visitation of death that allows for the
well-known chapters that follow.

The next chapter begins on an extended lyrical note, as the narrator stands on deck at dawn, eagerly awaiting the sighting of
Cerigo. The lyrical transports shift him from present to past, to the
rhetoric of Homeric epithets and to the age when the island was
called Cythera:

> Je l'ai vue ainsi, je l'ai vue: ma journée a commencé comme un
> chant d'Homère! C'était vraiment l'Aurore aux doigts de rose
> qui m'ouvrait les portes de l'Orient! Et ne parlons plus des au-
> rores de nos pays, la déesse ne va pas si loin. . . . Elle vient,
> elle approche, elle glisse amoureusement sur les flots divins
> qui ont donné le jour à Cythéreé . . . Mais que dis-je? devant
> nous, là-bas, à l'horizon, cette côte vermeille, ces collines em-
> pourprées qui semblent des nuages, c'est l'île même de Venus,
> c'est l'antique Cythère aux rochers de porphyre. . . . (64)

One might say that at this moment, as he salutes the island with a
citation in Greek, the narrator has escaped from personal memory
into the nostalgia of an ancient mythology, putting a cultural space,
rather than the breadth of the seas, between his present self and that
"doux et triste souvenir." But here this imaginative, rhetorical leap
collapses; the paragraph ends with a sentence that foreshadows the
next one:

> Aujourd'hui cette île s'appelle Cérigo et appartient aux Anglais.
> Voilà mon rêve . . . et voici mon réveil! Le ciel et la mer
> sont toujours là; le ciel d'Orient, la mer d'Ionie se donnent
> chaque matin le saint baiser d'amour; mais la terre est morte,
> morte sous la main de l'homme, et les dieux se sont envolés!
> Pour rentrer dans la prose, il faut avouer que Cythère n'a
> conservé de toutes ses beautés que ses rocs de porphyre, aussi
> triste à voir que de simples rochers de grès. Pas un arbre . . . je
> n'ai aperçu qu'un gentleman qui tirait aux bécasses et aux

pigeons, et des soldats écossais blonds et rêveurs, cherchant peut-être à l'horizon les brouillards de leur patrie. (64)

The narration of disillusion is produced by a structure of oppositions that is dominated by the duality of Past and Present. Opposed beneath the categories of Time we find Unchanging Nature/Changing Culture; Natural Harmony/Political Discord; Dream/Waking Reality; Possibility of Poetry/Necessity of Prose; Gods of Animism/ Englishmen of Imperialism. The list of oppositions goes beyond the material necessary for a contained psychological narrative concerning a subject's relation to memory, or the impossibility of escaping personal history through a flight into myth. Already the list contains political and historical values, and if Nerval writes that the animating gods of Cythera "se sont envolés," it is clearly because they have been driven away by the advent of modern man.

It is not surprising, then, that the sight of a corpse hanging from a gibbet—a scene presented two chapters later, after a digression on the powers of Venus Urania—provokes a narration in the form of a political allegory:

> Pendant que nous rasions la côte, avant de nous abriter à San-Nicolo, j'avais aperçu un petit monument, vaguement découpé sur l'azur du ciel, et qui, du haut d'un rocher, semblait la statue encore debout de quelque divinité protectrice . . . . Mais, en approchant davantage, nous avons distingué clairement l'objet qui signalait cette côte à l'attention des voyageurs. C'était un gibet, un gibet à trois branches, dont une seule était garnie. Le premier gibet réel que j'aie vu encore, c'est sur le sol de Cythère, possession anglaise, qu'il m'a été donné de l'apercevoir! (70–71)

The theme of disillusionment is overtaken here by political commentary: although a dual structure persists through the two-stage apprehension of the "petit monument," it is the centrality of the monument itself, and its revelation as the ironic antithesis of the anticipated monument, that enables the cadaver to become a figure for the fall of an entire mythos.

We might wonder what aspect of Nerval's narration of his own voyage to Cythera so strikes Baudelaire as in need of correction. On the one hand it may well smack of a nostalgia for a sunny Greek paganism, but on the other, the excursion to Cythera is ominously occasioned by death, laced with references to the chaste and mystical love inspired by the "higher" form of Aphrodite, and ends with a meditation on imperialism. This is not particularly strong stuff compared, for instance, to Leconte de Lisle's "Hypatie," in *Poèmes antiques,* where Jesus is called "Le vil Galiléen." Why should Baudelaire write and underscore "*l'incorrigible* Gérard" in the note accompanying his own version of such a voyage?

My question is essentially unanswerable, but I want to maintain it as a kind of backdrop against which to project some of the problems we will encounter in reading the versions of the poem. Let us turn first to the "Voyage" that Gautier received in 1852.[13]

As in the Nerval passage on the "petit monument," the motif of *approximation* provides the initial unifying key to reading this rather long poem. The title's assertion that we are concerned with a voyage frames the series of stanzas within the fiction of spatial motion, and, further, points at the possibility of *discovery* as the reward for the journey. The stanzaic structure itself adds to the creation of an incremental progress, since each stanza is a self-contained syntactic unit whose unity is reinforced by the closure of the rhyme schemes. The annunciatory force of the title, combined with the enclosed stanzaic form, predisposes the reader to construe the text as a narrative of discovery, as a travel toward truth.

The poem's way of relating that discovery can be divided into four parts. In stanzas 1 through 5, the presence of a somewhat naive speaker is established; he is bound toward the island of Cythera and sights it from the deck of a ship. Twice in these stanzas, the poem shifts from a stress on feeling to a stress on seeing. First the speaker's narration of shipboard ecstasy is interrupted by a question directly addressed to a more experienced traveler; the question results from the sudden sighting of the "île triste et noire" that turns out to be Cythera. The informant not only names the island, but describes it in a mock eulogy as the "Eldorado banal de tous les vieux garçons," and ends his intervention with the command "Regardez." The response of the speaker is not to look, however, but rather to launch into a nostalgic apostrophe to the island as the evergreen home of the spirit of love. This apostrophe builds upon its own rhetorical momentum to the point that it causes the one exception to my observation on the independent syntax of each stanza in the text: the fourth stanza spills into the fifth, as a second metaphorical possibility is offered for the effect of the universal adoration of the island. This literally gushing movement is stopped short by the declaration of lines 18 and 19; once again, seeing curtails the overflow of emotion. The opening section of the poem ends by fixing, through the iterative effect of a verb in the imperfect, the speaker's attention on an as yet ill-perceived object:

J'entrevoyais pourtant, un objet singulier.

What follows in the next five stanzas might be called a shifting of icons, from the myrtle of Venus (line 13) to the cypress of death (line 28). First, the speaker describes what he did not see, or rather denies the reader the delicate sensuality that might be presupposed by the *topos* of Cythera. The following stanzas (the poem's progress of approximation having brought us "assez près") then depict the hanging body of the man that we find in place of the living body of the priestess. The negative reversal from living woman to dead man is underscored by a series of contrasting echoes from the opening stanzas: the birds that had been the vehicles in comparisons of joy are now agents of destruction; the sunny light has been obscured by the black gibbet; the "fêtes du coeur" are now a literal *fête du corps,* while the "doux secrets" of the island are revealed to be the "délices" of the castrating birds rather than those of swooning lovers. The description of the hanged man does not end simply by inverting the sentimental expectations that we can ascribe to the speaker's naiveté, however; it displaces the very state of anticipation, by ending, in stanza 10, with the horde of eager earthbound "quadrupèdes" awaiting the further demise of the carrion.

The stanzas of description are followed by three successive apostrophes to the hanged man. There has been some acrimonious discussion about exactly what they all "mean" referentially.[14] For the moment I think it best to follow Bernard Weinberg, who, in his explication of the poem, suggests that a certain imprecision concerning "tes douleurs" and "les miennes" is advantageous: "It allows for concentration on the passion itself, on the suffering, rather than on accidental causes."[15] For the speaker, these apostrophes are acts of interpretation, and as such they recapitulate and then expand the prior trajectory of the poem. The first apostrophe invokes rather blankly a "habitant de Cythère," recapitulating the naiveté of the opening stanzas. The second addresses a "pauvre pendu muët," specifying again the nature of the voyage's revelation. In the third apostrophe, "devant toi, pauvre diable," the emphasis is laid on the specular fixity of the relationship between speaker and *pendu*: in this relationship, the interpreter is interpreted by that with which he identifies.

The final pair of stanzas constitutes a coda from which the speaker emerges in a strange apotheosis of disgust. The motif of the song—evoked by the disparaging comment of the informant, "Un pays fameux dans les chansons," by the "roucoulement eternel d'un ramier," and by the strophic text itself—is displaced upon "le ciel," as if only God might truly sing; "charmant" derives from the Latin *carmen*, or song. The sea reflects the sky in all its expansive and charming glory, while the speaker can reflect little more than his own reflection. That reflection, though, at least offers the comfort of letting one know what, and who, one is, for though the self is fixed and buried, it is also wrapped and bundled:

> Pour moi, tout était noir et sanglant désormais,
> Hélas! et j'avais comme en un suaire épais
> Le coeur enseveli dans cette allégorie.

The "allégorie" to which the speaker refers is constituted by the equation of self with scene—by the moralizing of the landscape to the point that it represents the self back to the interpreting subject. In that process of allegorization, the self recognizes itself as a stable image, or as what it might call a destiny. This is the thrust of the final stanza: having displaced the realm of song to the sky, the speaker can only croak out a pair of halfhearted apostrophes that are little more than exclamations. The first retells the story of how truth has been come upon in the form of a mirror:

Dans ton île, ô Venus, je n'ai trouvé debout
Qu'un gibet dégoûtant où pendait mon image.

The second takes the form of a prayer, but amounts to no more than
the prediction that in the future, as at the moment of enunciation, the
speaker will remain captivated by the image that represents him:

Oh Seigneur! donne-moi la force et le courage
De contempler mon coeur et mon corps sans dégoût.[16]

The last stanza contains a glaring and, to some readers, perhaps
awkward repetition of the words "dégoûtant" and "dégoût." The
repetition disappears in the later version, as we shall see, but we
ought to appreciate its function here rather than write it off as a
"mistake." First, it strongly unifies the voice of the speaker across
the space of two distinct exclamations, leaving no doubt that it is
under the sign of *dégoût* that the speaker has seen, and will go on
speaking, himself. By the same token, the repetition of *dégoût* in relation to both the sight of the gibbet and the act of self-contemplation
underscores the specular fixity of the speaker's identification: "tes
douleurs sont les miennes"; this is my image; it is disgusting and I
am disgusting; it is me.

   If the function of repetition is to stress fixity at the poem's end,
then it functions further to establish a contrast with another repetition, in the poem's opening stanza. There, an entire simile occurs
twice:

Mon coeur comme un oiseau s'envolait tout joyeux,
Et planait librement à l'entour des cordages,
Le navire roulait sous un ciel sans nuages,
Comme un oiseau qu'enivre un soleil radieux.

This is a strange reiteration of a figure, for it is not typical of
Baudelaire to run quickly dry of analogies. We might not only ask
why "comme un oiseau" occurs twice here, but ask as well why it
occurs *only* twice, instead of three, four, or more times? That is, the
repetition of the figure, and the resulting identification of heart

(self) with bird, and ship with bird, and self with ship, hint at a potentially endless chain of identifications—and thus a far-flung dispersion of the self—through the rhetoric of likening. In the poem, the flight of the bird-simile is stopped short by the sight of the sad, black island, but the potential for a limitless rhetorical bonding of self and world is nonetheless revealed through the repetition in the first stanza. And the failure of the figure "comme un oiseau" to repeat itself again and again results from the interruption of bliss by the faculty of vision. Thus the contrastive repetition of *dégoût* at the poem's end serves to bring into relief the tension between blissful dispersion of self and painful sighting of self that marked the poem's first stanzas, a tension ultimately resolved in favor of specular fixation. That resolution is dramatized by the progression of similes throughout the text, beginning with airy repetition—"comme un oiseau"—then, in the second moment of blissful discourse, turning to the ethereal—"comme un arôme"—but heading afterwards to the morbid and self-enclosing—"comme un cyprès," "comme un exécuteur," and "comme en un suaire épais."

The underscored tension between self-dispersion and self-definition, and the implicit progress of the voyage's movement from the former to the latter, keenly parallel the contrast between the infantile "pleasure-ego" and the mature ego, dominated by the reality principle, that Freud discusses in the first chapter of *Civilization and Its Discontents*. In that essay, as in "Voyage à Cythère," the discussion is motivated by the question of an "oceanic feeling." The notion of such a feeling had been put to Freud by Romain Rolland in the course of their correspondence, and Freud, claiming such a feeling, "as of something limitless, unbounded—as it were, 'oceanic'," to be foreign to his own experience, sets out to disclose the psychic genesis of that subjective state.[17]

In the course of a rather flinty analysis of the feeling, Freud proposes that this strange breakdown of the usual certainty concerning what elements constitute the "inside" and the "outside" of the self is in fact a regression to the state of infantile bliss, when an all-incorporating pleasure-ego does not yet see itself as distinct from the body of the mother. Since "in mental life nothing which has once been formed can perish," the mature self can nostalgically revert to the state that was prior to the constitution of the self as

a separate entity in a world of the "I" and the "not-I." The forma-
tion of the mature ego as a separate entity is a function of the domi-
nation of the pleasure principle by the reality principle.

> In this way, then, the ego detaches itself from the external
> world. Or, to put it more correctly, originally the ego includes
> everything, later it separates off an external world from itself.
> Our present ego-feeling is, therefore, only a shrunken residue
> of a much more inclusive—indeed, an all-embracing—feeling
> which corresponded to a more intimate bond between the ego
> and the world about it. If we may assume that there are many
> people in whose mental life this primary ego-feeling has per-
> sisted to a greater or less degree, it would exist in them side by
> side with the narrower and more sharply demarcated ego-
> feeling of maturity, like a kind of counterpart to it. In that case,
> the ideational contents appropriate to it would be precisely
> those of limitlessness and of a bond with the universe—the
> same ideas with which my friend elucidated the 'oceanic' feel-
> ing. (15)

Freud's critique of the "oceanic feeling" entails, then, a developmental scenario or fiction; he tells a tale about the self in terms of early
and later, primary and mature, stages of definition, enjoining the
reader to agree with his prior postulation that "normally, there is
nothing of which we are more sure than the feeling of our self, of
our own ego." Normally, that is, the conscious self may be traversed
by representatives of unconscious drives and desires—it may be invaded from the inside—but it maintains "clear and sharp lines of
demarcation" between the self and any "outside." The "oceanic
feeling" is not only enabled by a psychic capacity to drift backwards
toward memories of an infantile—unrealistic—bliss, but it also
poses a threat to the most normal, self-apparent boundary marker
by which the mature self orients itself in respect to the world;
whence the tension in Freud's first chapter between the mildly con-
descending tone in which he corrects a character whom we might
call *l'incorrigible* Romain Rolland, and the strongly authoritative tone
of his analytic performance. The "oceanic feeling" is merely a literary expansion upon a clearly understandable psychic phenomenon;

but it threatens to be, at the same time, a poetic sanction of madness. Freud wrote this first chapter as a separate piece, published in 1929, at a time when he had good reason to beware the possibility of sentimentalizing, from whatever political position, the dilution of individual consciousness.

Freud's rectifying deflation of the "oceanic feeling" that Rolland had brought to his attention offers sharp, though reductive, parallels to Baudelaire's deflation of the speaker of the "Voyage à Cythère." Both texts engage in a form of ventriloquism—Freud reporting on his friend's suggestion, and Baudelaire creating a suspiciously blissful voice only to subject it to what Weinberg calls "retrospective irony."[18] Both texts take as their opening position the proclamation of an "oceanic feeling"—quite literally in the case of the poem— that dilutes the boundaries between the subject of that feeling and the world about him; Rolland reportedly thematizes this notion, while Baudelaire's speaker implies it through the repetition of the bird simile. And both Freud and Baudelaire lead the subject of the "oceanic feeling" to the painful reality of the true position of the subject in the world—castration. In the Freudian text, "castration" is the sign of the status of the mature ego, cut off from the body of the mother, alone in a world of potential danger. In Baudelaire, the ultimate detail revealed in the depiction of the cadaver that is also the self-image is that Cytherean's loss of the "organ of love":

> L'organe de l'amour avait fait leurs délices,
> Et ces bourreaux l'avaient cruellement châtré.

Let us not hastily reduce Baudelaire's lines to no more than an intuitively informed "Freudian" sense of the world. A reader, for instance, who wishes to interpret *une poésie voyante* as a poetry based on a clear-sighted perception of moral predicaments will be quick to point out the pathos and irony that are densely evoked here: the destruction of the "organ of love" on the island of Venus, the transportation of *délices* from the realm of human sexual pleasure to the realm of inimical and natural forces that tear at the body, the invasion of the sunny pagan island by the dark image of sin and fallenness, all these negative reversals are present here, and all can be linked to a "syphilitic" consciousness of evil.[19] At the same time, however, a reader who assumes that the verbal structure of a text reflects, in part, a psychic process—regardless of whether that reader attributes the process to a speaker, to the writer, or even only to himself—will note that the castration of the hanged man appears as the final detail of Baudelaire's description, and that it appears to trigger the set of identifications that lead to the poem's end. For that reader, the castration of the *pendu* is a powerful image that enables the poem's speaker to stabilize and globalize his own, "proper" image, to "see" his past, present, and future in a representation, to arrest the "oceanic" leaking of self into an outside, and ultimately to "speak" the "Voyage" toward its destination. For that reader, a *poésie voyante* will be a poetry of specularity, and the double sense of *voyant*—both active and passive, clear-seeing and easily seen, insightful and gaudy—will only emphasize the problematics of self-representation by means of mirrors.[20] That reader would find the poem dramatizing one way of "getting yourself together" and would stress that, no matter how anguished the moment of revelation might be, it grants the speaker a stable sense of who he is. My two hypothetical readers would probably find themselves at odds over which conclusions can most pertinently be drawn from the "Voyage à Cythère"; my purpose at this point is not to advance either mode of reading the poem, but rather to suggest that both the socio-thematic and the Freudian approaches are plausible responses to *this* version of the poem. The question to be entertained later concerns whether either reading is adequate to the revised text that appears in *Les Fleurs du Mal.*

Between Freud's essay and Baudelaire's poem, there is a fourth parallel that remains to be considered. Both writers make it clear that they intend to correct a misled colleague. In both cases the object of correction is presented as perhaps too literary for his own good, and the prey of a regrettable nostalgia: Nerval is succinctly put forth as "*l'incorrigible* Gérard," with the knowledge that Gautier is only too familiar with his friend's interest in Greek and Egyptian mysticism, while Rolland is portrayed by Freud as one of the "exceptional few" worthy men of the time, then as "the friend whom I so much honour, and who himself once praised the magic of illusion in a poem."

But can we say that both texts operate as correctives to their intended object? That seems true enough in the case of Freud, for the essay often takes on an aggressively defensive tone. Indeed, his letters to Rolland show that he was far more troubled by the matter of the "oceanic feeling" than the essay would lead the reader to believe.[21] In the case of Baudelaire, however, the poem does not bear out the implicit goal of rectification that we find in the note to Gautier. The chapters of the *Voyage en Orient* that I have discussed tell of a failed attempt to flee the pain of personal memory; the "Voyage à Cythère" is structured around a similarly impossible flight. Nerval turns the story toward political allegory whereas Baudelaire tells more an allegory of the self, but he does not thereby correct any claim of Nerval's text. Nor does he engage Nerval in a theological debate over the redeeming value of Christianity: in the first place, Nerval's text eschews the theological in favor of the political; in the second, Baudelaire's text portrays a self bound within a sense of irremediable fallenness, far from the hope for redemption. As a corrective lesson, the poem simply fails. Whatever other parallels Freud's essay may offer us, this last is not one of them.

But Baudelaire does offer such corrections to Nerval—or at least to a certain figuration of him—in another text, the short essay "L'Ecole païenne," which was written shortly before the note to Gautier. In that rather furious text, full of ventriloquism, sarcasm, and a vague sense of panic, Baudelaire, without naming them, castigates: Nerval—"un homme qui a trop lu et mal lu Henri Heine et sa littérature pourrie de sentimentalisme matérialiste"; Gautier—"la plastique, cet affreux mot me donne la chair de poule, la plastique l'a empoisonné, et cependant il ne peut vivre que par ce poison"; and various others including, it would seem, himself—"la brûlante Sapho, cette patronne des hystériques."[22] The "patronne des hysteriques" would be, after all, the patron of *Les Lesbiennes*—the title that Baudelaire had long preferred for his planned volume of verse. And precisely because the essay is self-inclusive in its scope, it opens uneasily with a half-satirical dialogue between a *je* and a composite figure of a tipsy "pagan" poet. The debate begins over the question of whether revolution is necessarily anti-Christian.

—Mais, lui disais-je, qu'est-ce que le dieu Pan a de commun avec la révolution?

It quickly moves toward theology—it is a question of the truth of the mysterious announcement, reported in Plutarch, that "LE DIEU PAN EST MORT"—and ultimately toward the status of the anagogic level of allegorical interpretation, since Plutarch's story had come to be read, by the time of Rabelais, as the veridical presentiment of Christ's death and man's redemption.[23] The interlocutor, however, remains quite incorrigible, and the text takes on a shrill tone as the dialogue ends, turning immediately to the Nervalian figure, "un homme qui a trop lu et mal lu Henri Heine." In short, any corrective vigor aimed at Nerval seems to have been invested in this essay, along with a great deal of uncertainty about how poets, the poetic project, and the notion of "beauty" should situate themselves in relation to a world of poverty and revolution.

Thus the implicit intent to correct "*l'incorrigible* Gérard" that we find in the note to Gautier constitutes a displacement of that intent, a substitution of intent, or a screening of intent. This is not to say that Baudelaire is lying to Gautier, but rather that such screening may well serve the sender of the poem better than it may deceive the recipient. The screen of rectification serves as a ground against which the poem can be sent, spoken of, or thought about at all. We cannot know whether a written text of the poem existed before 1852, but we can know that when the poem is sent to Gautier, it carries an especial charge in Baudelaire's mind, that it is labeled as *voyante,* and that it is masked to him as a correction. And we can suspect that, since it does not effectively correct, its project is more akin to the constitution of a voice, of a lyric writing subject, in the midst of personal and historical ruins. At the same moment that history is repeating itself as farce, and that Baudelaire's situation has become a black comedy, the "Voyage à Cythère" first emerges as the declaration of an apparent poetic stance under the sign of *dégoût.*

We remember that Baudelaire writes to his mother with "des larmes de honte et de rage dans les yeux." The poem, in contrast, does not use bodily secretions as vehicles for externalizing anger, but instead as vehicles for "tasting" the sapidity of a stable inside:

> Je sentis à l'aspect de tes membres flottants,
> Comme un vomissement remonter vers mes dents
> Le long fleuve de fiel de mes douleurs anciennes;

It is the very acridity with which the self manifests itself that testifies to its reality, its presence in the image, and its self-presence by means of the image. An inside that is experienced as bitter, distasteful, or *dégoûtant* is nonetheless a reassuringly formulable inside. I would thus claim that Baudelaire has written out, in this earlier "Voyage," a poetic platform—not in the sense of an aesthetic manifesto, but in the sense of a solid ground from which the writer can conceive the poetic fiction of a voice. We can infer from the screening of his intent that the poem's operation is inadmissible to the man whose signature it bears, and that it must be masked as a gesture of rectification. This *poésie voyante*, however, surfaces in a situation that is marked, as Baudelaire seems to recognize in "L'Ecole païenne," more by anxiety hysteria than by the assured need to rectify a misled fellow poet.

Critical Paths

> (mon cerveau serait-il un miroir ensorcelé?)
> —*Fusées*

As I mentioned earlier, Baudelaire's reference to "*l'incorrigible* Gérard" in his note to Gautier is only one of two indications that the poet has Nerval in mind, in one way or another, when he sends the "Voyage à Cythère" to the *Revue de Paris*. And if the epithet "incorrigible" has informed the text with a corrective intention, the second reference to Nerval has led readers toward the specific object of correction. This reference is found in an epigraph or, more exactly, an outline for an epigraph that Baudelaire appended to the manuscript of his poem. It would appear to be no more than a note to an editor, and reads: "Le point de départ de cette pièce est quelques lignes de Gérard (*Artiste*) qu'il serait bon de retrouver." The word "*Artiste*" in parentheses names the journal in which Nerval's reports of his travels in the East first appeared serially, beginning in 1844. Those articles were the ones that Champfleury summarized in 1849, and which Nerval revised to form the *Voyage en Orient* in 1851.

The reference to a few lines in "L'Artiste" is, then, far less than clear, and the relative clause adding that it would be nice to find them only compounds the obscurity. In fact, it adds an almost ludic tone to the "epigraph," as if to propose a wild goose chase for a literary source. The potential playfulness of the final clause has been far overshadaowed, however, by the first words of this little note—"le point de départ." This *point de départ* implies, of course, a voyage, a trip, a progress. "Voyage" is already the title's primary framing device, asking that the poem be read in the spirit of the spiritual autobiography, as the progress of the pilgrim. The epigraphical note thus doubles this frame, frames that frame within itself, calling the "Voyage" a metavoyage of writing. By claiming that an (obscured) passage from Nerval is the "point" from which his writing has "departed," Baudelaire metaphorizes the writing of his text—or texts; we cannot know—so that the poem is presented as the destination of a literary excursion. Thus he seems to place his own act of writing squarely within a powerful conception of literary history, in which any such act marks an incrementally progressive event beyond the prior texts of a certain period or stage of consciousness.

This framing of the frame within itself has exercised considerable seductive power. As might any such gesture toward a source, it has appealed to an intense critical curiosity about where poems come from. That appeal can be appreciated by observing the eagerness of readers to repeat the metaphorics of the voyage as they tell their own tale of the text. There is no little excitement, for instance, in Antoine Adam's refutation of a different source-theory widely accepted prior to the publication of the 1852 manuscript:

> Baudelaire a lui-même indiqué, par une note jetée sur une copie autographe de ce poème, que "*Le Point de départ*" se trouvait dans quelques lignes de Nerval. Ces lignes se lisent en effet dans *L'Artiste* du 30 juin et du 11 août 1844 . . . .
>
> Ce point de départ certain rend probablement inutile un rapprochement qui a été proposé avec une page des *Adventures d'Arthur-Gordon Pym,* et du même coup il n'est plus interdit de placer la date de composition de ce poème avant la découverte de Poe, dans la période qui va de 1844 à 1852. Si l'on se laissait aller à tirer quelque conclusion de la langue et du style, on dirait que ces vers furent écrits plutôt vers 1844 que vers 1852.[24]

Adam's tone is triumphant—"Baudelaire lui-même . . . en effet . . . inutile . . . il n'est pas interdit"—and I have cited his note as an exemplary critical move that seizes on the phrase "point de départ" as a "certain" indicator within an apparently unproblematic epigraph. In the heat of the critical moment, the metaphoric value of the phrase is erased by Adam's desire to overcome those unnamed critics who have erroneously located the "point" and "moment" of the poem's inception. But, leaving aside the inevitable Oedipal struggles of critics and exigetes, one might begin to suspect that the critic who thus uses the metaphor for his own uses is simultaneously used by it as well, by virtue of his very insistence on it. It is as if the poem being read—and in this and the following cases, that poem is the canonical "Voyage" of 1857—intensifies concern for where one is coming from and going to.

Adam is not alone in capitalizing on the note's expansion of the voyage metaphor to include the process of creation. Enid Starkie, Baudelaire's most faithful biographer, repeats the phrase more cautiously than Adam, but employs it conclusively when she does reiterate it. She is arguing for a date of composition different from Adam's, pointing out that Baudelaire's knowledge of the content of the Nerval articles was not necessarily a direct and immediate one. It could have been mediated and delayed through the novelist Champfleury, who summarized the passage in an appreciation of Nerval's work in March, 1849. Starkie writes that Baudelaire

> had been a close friend of Champfleury since 1845, and he may well have read his article on publication—it is certain that he must have known it—and the subject was one that would strike his imagination forcibly, and with special significance, when he fell ill [with a recurrent attack of the syphilis that he had thought cured] at Dijon. This makes it probable that the poem was not written in 1844 as has often been suggested because of the appearance of de Nerval's article in June that year.[25]

Starkie wants to make a case for the possibility that the poem was written after the failed Revolution of 1848, during the poet's stay in Dijon, at a time of severe distress which she calls "the slough of despond." It is from this personal backwater that the poem-ship sets forth, she claims: "That is the point of departure for Baudelaire's poem." The biographer is not simply repeating the use of a certain phrase by her subject. By rooting the poem in a particularly desperate moment in Baudelaire's life, she is attenuating its violence by resorting to biographical anecdote—pleading extenuating circumstances, as it were, at the time of its writing. Her gesture of attenuation repeats the implicit intent of Baudelaire's epigraphical note to Gautier, and it does so through the metaphor of the "point of departure" by trying to bestow upon the text a biographical origin that accounts for it.

Baudelaire's ascription of a "point of departure"—his framing his "Voyage" within a metavoyage of writing—permits Adam to assert the truth of the poem's paternal origin, while allowing Starkie to make the maternal gesture of protecting the poet from the violence of his language by asserting the overriding value of his sincerity. By capitalizing on the poet's note, both the editor and the biographer profit by having a story to tell about the text.

Both their stories, however much motivated by the poet's repetition of the voyage metaphor in his note to Gautier, are relatively restrained, in the sense that they attempt to fix only the "point" where the poem has its textual or psychological source. Along with the restrained efforts of Adam and Starkie, there exists a more global narrative about the trip of this text in literary history. The path of the less restrained critical voyage ends beyond the Baudelaire poem itself, to arrive at Hugo's poem, "Cérigo," from Book V of *Les Contemplations*. According to this story, Baudelaire sets out to correct Nerval's supposed paganism, taking as his theme the discovery of corruption, mortality, and sin at the symbolic site of desire. Then, when the "Voyage à Cythère" is finally published, in the *Revue des deux mondes* in June, 1855, Hugo reads it and immediately composes a reply, his own correction of Baudelaire's correction. In this vein, P. Maury in 1925 contrasted the two poems thus:

Chez Baudelaire, c'est le poème du péché, de la souffrance expiatrice et de la prière qui sauve; chez Hugo, le poème de la vieillesse consolée, rajeunie par une conception plus haute de l'amour.[26]

Another critic, writing at around the same time, composed a brief, sentimental narrative to account for Hugo's motive in correcting the "Voyage":

> Il oublia le mal que Baudelaire avait dit de lui jadis; il ne vit dans ces strophes qu'une pensée à rectifier, une âme à consoler, une vérité à affirmer. On peut croire aussi que Victor Hugo n'était pas fâché de faire la leçon à un confrère qui ne l'avait point ménagé.[27]

The direct linking of three authors in a series of corrective texts provides a strong argument for a notion of simple and direct intertextual influence within a concept of the history of literature as a progressive enterprise. The story of the Nerval-Baudelaire-Hugo connection surrounding and, in a sense, surpassing the "Voyage à Cythère" was most effectively promulgated, though not invented, by Crépet and Blin in their notes to the critical edition of *Les Fleurs du Mal* (Corti, 1942). Since the publication of that work, Léon Cellier has reconsidered the question of a linear relation among the texts of the three authors. He has performed parallel readings of Nerval's 1844 articles and "Cérigo," showing Hugo's poem to contain a preponderance of echoes from the language of those early articles in *L'Artiste*. He is led to infer that Hugo had been working from those articles well before he ever laid eyes on Baudelaire's poem, if indeed he saw it at all before completing "Cérigo." Cellier's discussion leads him to conclude that any interplay between the two poems is the result of mere coincidence, rather than a relation of causality. He ends as follows:

> Concluons: si l'historien n'écrit pas une vie romancée, il lui est impossible d'aboutir à la moindre certitude relativement à ce problème. Beaucoup de bruit pour rien![28]

Much ado about nothing! Cellier's lexical analysis is carefully performed, and his conclusion masterfully put. He reveals the foibles of earlier readers who had been led to draw other conclusions that had amounted to a small fable of how "Un Voyage à Cythère" was positioned within a certain history of writing. On the other hand,

Cellier's analysis closes itself without trying to explore the possibility that the poem has invited its readers to indulge in such fables. Writing off their efforts with a masterful remark like "much ado about nothing" implies that one man is a better scholar than others, but avoids at the same time any possibility of speculating on the critical assumptions and desires that may lead to the writing of a tale of causality and teleology, particularly in relation to this poem. We are left to wonder if it is only another mere coincidence that this poem has given rise to a multiplicity of critical narratives designed to formulate its voyage as a simple trajectory. Why have a gaudy (*voyant*) epigraph about a *point de départ* and a pair of close dates of publication attracted readers to offer specific origins and destinations for this particular "Voyage"? Might not the text of "Un Voyage à Cythère" play some sort of unsettling role in generating the desire for all this stabilizing "ado"?

Cellier's parting shot, "beaucoup de bruit pour rien," has a certain brutal force in its scholarly context, and it is that very brusqueness that draws our attention. His remark has all the resonance of the abrupt denegation "it was really nothing," which Heidegger exploits in his discussion of *Angst* in *Being and Time*. "Really nothing," "noise for nothing," or "ado about nothing" can all serve as denials of the reality of the object of anxiety:

> When anxiety has subsided, then in our everyday way of talking we are accustomed to say that 'it was really nothing.' And *what* it was, indeed, does get reached ontically by such a way of talking. Everyday discourse tends towards concerning itself with the ready-to-hand and talking about it. That in the face of which anxiety is anxious is nothing ready-to-hand within-the-world.[29]

"Nothing" is really what anxiety is about: the cliché formulates, in casual language, the ontological revelation of anxiety, which is the state of mind resulting from Dasein's intuition that its only Being is a Being-possible, a Being-towards—a Being that cannot coincide with itself at any given "present." Cellier's dismissive remark may well put a few scholars in their places, but it may also, by admitting that "nothing" is what their work was "for," allow us to suspect that

"Un Voyage à Cythère" is a text that elicits a certain anxiety in those who read it. In other words, Cellier gestures towards a reading project—that of Adam, Maury, *et al.*—that is motivated by an anxious concern to overcome a manifest negativity, a nothing, circulating in the text of the poem. Their *bruit pour rien* has consisted in locating points of departure and arrival for the text, and in using those points to weave a narrative framework around the poem by means of giving it a history. Rather than dismiss this "noise," I want to take it as a symptom—as a defensive reaction called forth by the text. Let us then turn our attention to the revised, published text of 1857, to discover how that text, in comparison to the earlier one we have already discussed, works to complicate the notion of its origin or originality, and to undercut its own narrative process.

Revision and Decomposition

> Le goût immodéré de la forme pousse à des
> désordres monstrueux et inconnus.
> –"L'Ecole païenne"

The text that appears in *Les Fleurs du Mal* has undergone many changes in detail, and its title has picked up an indefinite article. But it is still composed of fifteen stanzas; the rhyme scheme and rhyme words remain unchanged; and the incremental progress of the poem from the "oceanic" to "disgust" appears to have been maintained. It is, then, "essentially" the same poem: yet the changes in detail will allow me to suggest that the revised text calls into question the very notion of "essence" by foregrounding the power of the detail. My reading will not, however, insist that "Un Voyage à Cythère" exists as a "verbal icon" self-sustained by the tensions of ambiguity and irony. I wish instead to read toward a palpable negativity—a noise-provoking nothing—that works in this text against the palimpsest of the earlier version. This is not to say that the two versions I deal with can be enclosed in a two-part structure of a "before" and "after": on the one hand, Baudelaire's epigraphical reference to Nerval suggests that he conceives his "Voyage" always to be an aftereffect; on the other hand, the later text initiates reading problems that are enlivened by turning to the earlier version. "The" text, in effect, resides in the relation between two versions of the "same" poem.

Let us begin with the issue of narrativity. Bernard Weinberg begins his lengthy explication of "Un Voyage à Cythère" by stating: "Most apparent among the structural bases in this poem is the narrative line."[30] This means, he continues, that the poem "recounts a number of successive moments or episodes in a voyage, and it is the story that provides the chronological continuity." Of course any "story" provides a chronological continuity of some sort, in that any *sjuzet* provides a *fabula;* that is, any narration of events, even if it does not narrate events in their chronological sequence, refers to such a sequence and provides it eventually. But it is not really "chronological continuity" that Weinberg wants the "story" to "provide"; the chronological continuity that he affirms is in fact a mask for a prior continuity that he wants to be able to assume: a sufficient continuity of discourse to enable him to posit the function called "the speaker" of the poem. But as Weinberg performs a résumé of the poem's narrative line to begin his explication, we find him resorting to an agentless, passive voice at first, then a muddle of pronouns in his synopsis:

> Then the event: an island *is sighted,* a question *is asked* about its identity, an answer *is given* . . . . As the voyagers approach, *they* describe the island as it appears to them, . . . and *the speaker* begins to perceive something on the island: 'J'entrevoyais . . . un objet.' . . . *They* come closer, and *he* then sees it clearly: 'voila qu'en rasant la cote . . . . *Nous* vîmes que c'était un gibet . . . .' He next describes what was going on on the island. . . . *The speaker* addresses the hanged man. . . . In a summary statement at the end, *he* compares the episode with *his* feelings about it. . . .'[31]

The awkwardness of expression in the résumé results from a certain tension between the plethora of agents that are either pronominalized or erased, and the attempt to isolate a single, unifying function called "the speaker." It is, of course, a conventional expectation that a lyric poem contain, and be contained by, such a function. And the résumé cited above would be pertinent to an explication of the

manuscript version of the poem which Baudelaire wrote out in
1852, the version that begins as follows:

> Mon coeur, comme un oiseau, s'envolait tout joyeux
> Et planait librement à l'entour des cordages.
> Le navire roulait sous un ciel sans nuages,
> Comme un oiseau qu'enivre un soleil radieux.
>
> Quelle est cette île triste et noire? C'est Cythère,
> Me dit-on. Un pays fameux dans les chansons.
> Eldorado banal de tous les vieux garçons.
> Regardez, après tout, c'est une pauvre terre.
>
> Ile des doux secrets et des fêtes du coeur.
> De l'antique Venus. . . .

Compare the earlier text with the one that appears in the 1857 *Fleurs
du Mal,* and begins:

> Mon coeur, comme un oiseau, voltigeait tout joyeux
> Et planait librement à l'entour des cordages;
> Le navire roulait sous un ciel sans nuages,
> Comme un ange enivré d'un soleil radieux.
>
> Quelle est cette île triste et noire? —C'est Cythère,
> Nous dit-on, un pays fameux dans les chansons,
> Eldorado banal de tous les vieux garçons.
> Regardez, après tout, c'est une pauvre terre.
>
> —Ile des doux secrets et des fêtes du coeur!
> De l'antique Venus. . . .[32]

If we concentrate for the moment only on those changes which
affect the function of a speaker, we find that the change from *me* to
nous in line 6 is the most obvious one. What seems at first to be a
single voice in the text becomes pluralized and fragmented by the
narrative interjection "nous dit-on." Simultaneously, the pronoun
on, so elastic in its possible reference, which can be read in the early

version as referring to an unspecified but single interlocutor, becomes more plausibly plural when brought up against the *nous* of
the revision. Thus what appeared at first to evoke an exchange between two voyagers, the one naive and the other a more experienced traveler, appears in the revision to set the stage for exchanges
between an indeterminate number of speakers.

The later text has not merely undergone lexical changes, moreover; it has had added to it a set of purely typographical devices—
the dashes that appear above in lines 5 and 9. Such dashes do
not have a rigidly fixed meaning in poetry, nor even within the
Baudelairean corpus, but their function in this poem is made clear
by their first occurrence:

> Quelle est cette île triste et noire? —C'est Cythère. . . . (5)

Clearly the dash indicates a change of speaker, voice, or interlocutor
when it occurs in this line. At the beginning of line 9 it again separates voices, indicating the end of one speaker's jaded representation
of Cythera and the beginning of another speaker's fantastic one. Insofar as we limit ourselves to discussing the opening lines of the
poem, the dashes do not create a terrible problem for the commen-
tator who would privilege a particular voice within the poem. But if
the dashes function easily at the beginning to underline the parts of
a dramatic prologue, then they must function equivocally to undermine the possibility of reading the last lines of the text as an individual paroxysm of despair, guilt, and prayer. Compare the end of the
1852 text with that of the version that Weinberg is in the process of
reading as a univocal narrative:

> 1852 Pauvre pendu muet, tes douleurs sont les miennes.
>   Je sentis à l'aspect de tes membres flottants,
>   Comme un vomissement remonter vers mes dents
>   Le long fleuve de fiel de mes douleurs anciennes;
>
>   Devant toi, pauvre diable au souvenir si cher,
>   J'ai senti tous les becs et toutes les mâchoires
>   Des corbeaux lancinants et des panthères noires
>   Qui jadis aimaient tant à triturer ma chair.

Le Ciel était charmant, la mer était unie.
Pour moi, tout était noir et sanglant désormais,
Hélas! et j'avais comme en un suaire épais
Le coeur enseveli dans cette allégorie.

Dans ton île, ô Vénus, je n'ai trouvé debout
Qu'un gibet dégoûtant où pendait mon image.
Oh Seigneur! donnez-moi la force et le courage
De contempler mon coeur et mon corps sans dégoût.

1857   Ridicule pendu, tes douleurs sont les miennes!
Je sentis, à l'aspect de tes membres flottants,
Comme un vomissement, remonter vers mes dents
Le long fleuve de fiel de mes douleurs anciennes.

Devant toi, pauvre diable au souvenir si cher,
J'ai senti tous les becs et toutes les mâchoires
Des corbeaux lancinants et des panthères noires
Qui jadis aimaient tant à triturer ma chair.

—Le ciel était charmant, la mer était unie;
Pour moi tout était noir et sanglant désormais,
Hélas! et j'avais, comme en un suaire épais,
Le coeur enseveli dans cette allégorie.

Dans ton île, ô Vénus! je n'ai trouvé debout
Qu'un gibet symbolique où pendait mon image . . .
—Ah! Seigneur! donnez-moi la force et le courage
De contempler mon coeur et mon corps sans
      dégoût! (45–60)

The earlier text might be susceptible to an intensely moral and moralizing reading, for there is little question that the continuity of
voice needed for such a reading can be inferred by the reader. The
revised text, however, breaks that necessary continuity almost per-
versely by means of no more than a few purely typographical inser-
tions: two dashes and an ellipsis. It is almost as if the text finally
published in *Les Fleurs du Mal* were out to remind us to what an

extent "voice" is a mere construction in a written text—a construction that a few dots and dashes on a page can begin to undo. Those simple marks on the page possess a power so potentially insidious that they have been at times completely overlooked or denied by editors. Adrien van Bever is blind to them when he notes the variants of the "Voyage" in his 1925 edition of *Les Fleurs du Mal,* for example. A similar oversight occurs in the critical edition of Jacques Crépet and Georges Blin—the edition whose notes endorse most enthusiastically the story of a corrective series of texts among Nerval, Baudelaire, and Hugo. The latter example gives grounds for suggesting that the desire to create a linear narrative about the poem reflects, and is in turn reflected by, the desire to maintain a spurious univocity within the text at hand. Insofar as the inscription of the *tirets* during the process of revision might radically complicate the narrative possibilities of the text, the dashes must be discreetly repressed by readers who position themselves as narratees of the "Voyage," and narrators of its origins. Other readers who, like Weinberg, claim less interest in literary history, but who wish at least as strongly for the text to originate from a privileged and unified psychological construct called "the speaker," become tangled in forced and awkward phraseology in telling the story they would like the poem to be telling with them. Baudelaire's revision of the "Voyage" has called into question the possibility of making travel the analogon of self-discovery, and of proposing vision as the model for identity. Or, at the least, he has caused the text to foreground the role of the reader's desire if such models and analogies are to be put forth.

Does that mean that this text is without a tale? What are we to make of a revision that has undermined the vision of a monadic self's travel to a "moment of truth"? Of a text that fragments its finale into a polyphony? The few changes that we have so far considered have already resulted in a new poem, more opaque and elusive than the earlier one. Whatever story is being told here looks more like a debate than a self-enclosed revelation—or a self-revealing enclosure.

The Peculiar Absolute

> Car, certes, je croirais faire un sacrilège en
> appliquant le mot: extase à cette sorte de
> décomposition.
> — *Fusées*

In the revised text, the project for an epigraph to Nerval has been abandoned: the space between its title and its opening line remains blank. What, then, of its *point de départ?* Does the erasing of the epigraph imply no such point, or rather a plurality of departures? One could assert that the disappearance of a dedication to Nerval has a thematic relation to the revision of the text. After all, Baudelaire has worked changes that result in a shift to a different set of problems, to the extent that the poem might now stand disengaged from its Nervalian "source." The absence of dedication might attest to a growth of a kind of poetic pride in the poet, who now decides to let his poem stand alone in all of its newly acquired opacity. If the earlier epigraph had established Nerval in the position of a textual Father, then one might even suggest that the lack of epigraph here parallels the fragmentation of voice at the climactic moment of prayer in the poem, disclosing the desire to occult Fathers completely.

Or one might speculate that, by the time he is preparing his poems for *Les Fleurs du Mal,* Baudelaire has another poet on his mind: Victor Hugo. In 1852, Hugo had not yet become the heroic exile-of-the-islands: he was in exile, to be sure, but only in Brussels. By 1857, his image as French letters' own Napoleon in exile had been well established by *Les Contemplations,* and we find Baudelaire noting in his *Fusées*:

> —Hugo pense souvent à Prométhée. Il s'applique un vautour imaginaire sur une poitrine qui n'est lancinée que par les moxas de la vanité. Puis l'hallucination se compliquant, se variant, mais suivànt la marche progressive décrite par les médecins, il croit que par un *fiat* de la Providence, Sainte-Hélène a pris la place de Jersey.
>
> Cet homme est si peu élégiaque, si peu éthéré, qu'il ferait horreur même à un notaire.

Hugo-Sacerdoce a toujours le front penché; —trop penché
pour rien voir, excepté son nombril.[33]

It is very possible that the figure of the solitary victim on the island of Cythera had produced deep and ambivalent resonances in
Baudelaire, and that his revision of the poem conflates the "pauvre
pendu"—now a "ridicule pendu"—of the earlier, Nervalian version
with the overpowering and somewhat pompous figure now cut by
Hugo. He may have erased the reference to Nerval in order to allow
a more contemporary but more oblique reference to Hugo to be
glimpsed by the reader. But if Hugo does partake of the new epithet
ridicule, then the multi-voiced reactions to the sighting of the overdetermined image of the hanged and decomposing cadaver can only
add to the already complex question of the place that Hugo occupies
in Baudelaire's writing.

Whether we interpret the disappearance of the Nervalian epigraph as a stance of poetic pride or as a gesture of poetic hostility,
we are led to problems of influence and motive, and thus returned to
the notion of origins, or *points de départ.* As we turn to this, the second of the two critical obsessions this poem has generated, we will
be seeking possible answers not only to the question of the origin
of the text, but to the questions that the text poses about originality
and writing. And we will continue to interrogate the revisions
worked on the earlier text.

I want to focus attention on four stanzas in particular, because the
changes made in them offer a clear pattern, and because these stanzas
form the representation of what is *really* to be seen on the island of
Cythera. Having negated the imagery of a certain tradition in order
to open a space for its own imagination, the poem leads us to its
catastrophic vision. I will present the two versions of the text stanza
by stanza:

1852   Mais voilà qu'en rasant la côte d'assez près
       Pour troubler les oiseaux avec nos voiles blanches
       Nous vîmes que c'était un gibet à trois branches
       Du ciel se détachant en noir comme un cyprès.

1857   *idem*

1852   De féroces oiseaux perchés sur leur pâture
        Dévoraient avec rage un pendu déjà mur,
        Et chacun jusqu'aux yeux plantait son bec impur
        Dans tous les coins saignants de cette pourriture.

1857   De féroces oiseaux perchés sur leur pâture
        Détruisaient avec rage un pendu déjà mur,
        Chacun plantant, comme un outil, son bec impur
        Dans tous les coins saignants de cette pourriture;

1852   Les yeux étaient deux trous, et du ventre effondré
        Les intestins pesants lui coulaient sur les cuisses,
        L'organe de l'amour avait fait leurs délices,
        Et ces bourreaux l'avaient cruellement châtré.

1857   Les yeux étaient deux trous, et du ventre effondré
        Les intestins pesants lui coulaient sur les cuisses,
        Et ses bourreaux, gorgés de hideuses délices,
        L'avaient à coups de bec absolument châtré.

1852   Sous les pieds un troupeau de jaloux quadrupèdes
        Le museau relevé tournoyait et rôdait;
        Une plus grande bête au milieu s'agitait,
        Comme un exécuteur entouré de ses aides.

1857   Sous les pieds, un troupeau de jaloux quadrupèdes,
        Le museau relevé, tournoyait et rôdait;
        Une plus grande bête au milieu s'agitait
        Comme un exécuteur entouré de ses aides. (25–40)

The changes in these stanzas attenuate the violence of the initial lines so that an aura of suspense is created, concentrating violence toward their end. The revised stanzas, in other words, impose a direction upon their violence, leading to a final localization of it in the awful spectacle of line 36. The opening remains unchanged, making the transition between the negation of the sentimental Cythera and the representation of the actual Cythera by shifting the optics of the mimesis from the horizontal course of the "jeune prêtresse" to a sudden glance upwards—up the mast of the ship, seen from the deck, looking up that mast at the sails and the birds circling above. Then, with dizzying speed, the sight line swerves down and across to the shore, to arrive at the gibbet and its revelatory burden. The stanza serves in both cases as a hinge between the erotically mobile female body, which exists only as an imaginary, textual figure, and the morbidly static hanged man, whose eruption in the text is lent symbolic force by this vertical scanning of mast and sails. But our encounter with that cadaver has become modulated in the process of revision. In the second stanza cited, "dévoraient" is replaced by "détruisaient," and thus the primal force of the notion of incorporation is replaced by a more global, technical, and distanciating verb; the action of the birds begins to be reduced to an impersonal matter of technics. The mediating power of the technical, and thus the decreased stress on the animus of the birds, is underscored by the weakening of the verb "plantait" to the participle "plantant," and then specified by the introduction of the simile "comme un outil" to replace the frenzied adverbial phrase "jusqu'aux yeux." The second stanza undergoes considerable revision, aimed at effacing the frenzy of the birds, so that their ultimate act of destruction wreaked upon the cadaver can surface with all the more shocking effect.

The bringing-to-light of the shocking details is accomplished in the third of the stanzas cited. There, the process of delayed revelation, and the concomitant focusing of violence, continue through the revision. The structure of the stanza, at first a run-on list of four clauses symmetrically linked in the pattern A + B, C + D, becomes asymmetrical: A + B, + C, where "C" is now a simple sentence that comprises the second half of the stanza. The shift from four to three clauses is made by displacing the initial phrase of line 4 of the early version, "Et ces (ses) bourreaux," to the beginning of line 3, resulting in a series of clauses where each succeeding clause is longer, and thus of higher value, than the one before. At the same time, the syntax of the third and longest clause functions to create the maximum space between subject, "bourreaux," and predication, "châtré." The expansion, in other words, serves to delay theatrically the degree of the cadaver's mutilation, doubling the time of anticipation before the final, horrific detail appears.

The expansion of the earlier text's fourth line results also in the elimination of its third line, erasing the euphemistic mention of the penis in the phrase "l'organe de l'amour." What is the effect of this erasure? "L'organe de l'amour" serves to create a certain local irony when it is destroyed on the island of Cythera, but as a euphemism for a specifiable body part, it also locates and domesticates that organ in the realm of the boudoir. Thus the penis—which we have come to think of as an age-old locus of identity in a binary sexual logic of either/or, as the measure of family authority, as the guarantor of the deep voice of rational speech, and as the hyper-cathected narcissistic mirror of manhood—was restricted by the earlier text to being the simple agent of copulation. The later text erases the good speech (*eu* + *pheme*) of the earlier version in the same gesture by which it fragments its own good speech into a polylogue. It is as if the earlier version's loss of a penile object is extrapolated, in the later text, into the loss of a phallic presence—both in relation to the body of the cadaver at hand, and in relation to the text of the poem itself. Which is to say that the violence of the representation of castration in the later text, and the fragmentation of the speaker's voice, exist in parallel with one another. If the revised text has turned a unity of voice into polyphony, it has done so in conjunction with a revision of its representation of castration: a revision that must be now read in greater detail.

The process of delay and suspense that we have observed at work throughout these four stanzas now becomes most acutely focused. In the extended space between the subject ("bourreaux") and the predication ("châtré") of the last two lines, we encounter a series of increasingly lurid phrases which heighten the anticipation for, but postpone the arrival at, the completion of the verb phrase. First, the subject of that verb phrase is personified as *bourreaux*, and the delayed charge of animus that we saw previously erased through technics now descends upon the birds, implying conscious malice on the part of the agent. The victim's helplessness, as well as the macabre formality of the entire event, are evoked at this point, and not before. This, in turn, prepares the context for the scene described in the following stanza, where a certain animal will be likened to an "exécuteur." Next, the line is completed by an adjectival phrase, "gorgés de hideuses délices," evoking excess not only lexically but metrically as well, since it makes the placement of the classical caesura awkward yet does not allow itself to be convincingly split to form a Romantic alexandrine either. The latter division is challenged by the syntactic unity of "de hideuses délices," a unity that is reinforced by the hammering alliteration of the phrase; the acoustic quality of the alliteration in turn stresses the violence involved in the excess of torture. Then, as the fourth line begins, the auxiliary verb and its pronominal object are offered only to be separated from the complementary participle by an adverbial phrase, "à coups de bec," which operates acoustically (takuəbɛk) in much the same way as the phrase before it, miming the process of laceration with its staccato occlusives. At last we arrive at the completed predication, "absolument châtré"; the voiceless /p/, fricative /s/, liquid /l/, and nasal /mã/ of the intensifying adverb contrast with the two preceding alliterative series to slide the hemistich to its conclusion.

Comparing the two versions of this moment in the text leads us initially to conclude that the changes wrought in revision result in a careful progression of successively more violent verses, playing the reader's sense of horror against his sense of curiosity on the way to the poem's most shocking, sensitive truth. And yet there is a curious element in the public unveiling of this private horror. If, for example, the other revisions can be recuperated under the sign of anticipation, the same cannot be said of the rewriting of "cruellement" as "absolument." To what end does the negation of affect work, when the more neutral adverb is substituted for the former? If "absolument" would correct a cloying identification with the victim, or an overindulgent moral condemnation of natural events, it nevertheless leads to a peculiar question: how do we read *absolute* castration? That is, can there be conceived a partial castration, opposed to which absolute castration will make sense of itself? If there *is* a difference, how much of the object that structures difference (for little Hans, for instance)[34] must disappear before the difference becomes apparent? But it is not simply a question of logic. If Baudelaire had written "complètement châtré," our interrogation of the phrase might end only with a somewhat facetious musing about what constitutes the measure of that completeness. But although "absolument" shares a received sense with "complètement," it is distinguished by deriving from the Latin *absolvere,* which means to loosen from, to make loose, to set free, to detach, or to untie. In the phrase "absolument châtré," as distinct from such plausible substitutes as "complètement châtré" or "totalement châtré," the fact of castration is marked and remarked, reinscribed in the adverb, incisively—and without cruelty.

The sedimented redundancy sets the phrase to turning about itself, dulling the cutting edge of its meaning by cutting over again, by overcutting. As a result, the apparently careful revisions of the preceding lines create a heightened expectation that is met, not by a full truth, but by a truth that is dizzyingly overfull—that seems to mean too much or too little, or both. Castration, when it finally appears, is presented hyperbolically; the question to be pursued is not that of complete/partial castration, but that of a doubled and duplicitous representation of castration.

Before we address this question directly and abstractly, we might briefly comment on the fourth of the stanzas cited above, in order to give both the question and its pursuit further context. In that stanza we are told that an expectant horde of earthbound beasts impatiently awaits the further demise of the cadaver. The changes made to the revised version amount to details in punctuation that serve to create pauses in the first two lines while allowing the last two to continue uninterrupted as a single long thought. That thought concerns a mysterious figure, "une plus grande bête," who arises in the midst of the horde "comme un exécuteur."

Now the French "exécuteur" can refer both to the executioner who dispenses with a victim and the executor who disburses his estate. Our reading of the word in this text must be guided, on the one hand, by the prior personification of the birds as "bourreaux," leading us to stress the most directly aggressive aspect of the menagerie. Insofar as he is an "executioner," the "plus grande bête" reiterates all the excessive violence of the "bourreaux," with the result that the reader's sympathy is directed away from him and toward the hapless victim. On the other hand, the rewriting of "cruellement" as "absolument" has erased an instance of sympathetic identification with that victim, inscribing instead a doubled mutilation. The repetitive intensity of the phrase "absolument châtré" creates an affective ambiguity at the very least in relation to the victim—making the reader hesitate between readings of the description as sympathetic and as downright sadistic. In other words, the locus of the text's sympathy becomes multiple at this point, erasing a simple identification with the victim in favor of a plurality of identifications—with victim and executioners alike. (One is reminded of a sentence from *Mon coeur mis à nu,* speculating on the pleasure of alternating between the roles of victim and executioner.) In the light of that possible plurality of identifications, one might go so far as to read the horde of "jealous quadrupeds" as a generation of post-Hugolian poets among whom one stands out as both executioner and executor, effacing the monumentality of Hugo through a certain "poésie voyante." One might even claim that the identity of the executor of the estate of the past is spelled out in the fantasmatic link among "exécuteur," "bourreaux," and "oiseaux," marking the "plus grande bête" as a *beau de l'air.* Thus the "inhabitant of Cythera" would be conflated with the exiled Hugo, the emperor-poet of the *Fusées,* and the rewritten "Voyage" would become an allegory of a poetic patricide. And there are good grounds for including that possibility in our reading of the text.

But to give oneself up completely to the temptation to rewrite the allegory of the rewritten text would involve also blinding oneself to the way the revised text's polyphony ironizes *any* allegorical reading, indeed, any impulse to allegory. As we have seen above, the imposition of the *tirets* at the poem's end invites us to assume that a different voice erupts in line 53 to exclaim:

> —Le ciel était charmant, la mer était unie;
> Pour moi tout était noir et sanglant désormais,
> Hélas! et j'avais, comme en un suaire épais,
> Le coeur enseveli dans cette allégorie.
>
> Dans ton île, ô Vénus! je n'ai trouvé debout
> Qu'un gibet symbolique où pendait mon image. . . .

And then still a different voice interjects, ultimately:

> —Ah! Seigneur! donnez-moi la force et le courage
> De contempler mon coeur et mon corps sans dégoût!

The first of the two voices equates allegorizing with being buried alive. Because of the dash that creates a crucial distance between this equation and the act of personal identification—"tes douleurs sont les miennes"—that precedes it, these six lines begin to emerge as a reaction to, or critique of, the mirroring that has just taken place. Further, the fragmentation of voice multiplies the deictic function of the phrase "cette allégorie": whereas the fiction of a unified voice would have the deixis pointing unequivocally beyond the text's enunciation, toward the *pauvre pendu* as the self's analogy, the pluri-vocalization of the poem allows that deixis to focus on the text's mo-bilization of *allégorie* as the process of self-mirroring.[35] Allegory, this remote voice proclaims, is an entombment, suggesting that the alle-gorization of experience is an act by which the self seeks to ground itself in a universe of meaning, but in which the self is not so much grounded as it is lost. The self finds its meaning through a reading of alterity, only to discover its identity residing in the other, given to the self as the other; represented. This paradox of identification is isolated by the punctuation of the revised text so that the "voice" of lines 53–58 can do no more than proclaim the alienating effect of the predicament; it both upholds the terrible power of the "gibet symbolique" to represent a self, and recognizes that representation as a deathly monumentalization.[36] It can contrast the charm of the sky and unity of the sea—natural foci of untroubled self-identity— to the ontological gap inherent in the dual relationship of self and counterpart, and it can thus critically formulate the contradiction that underlies the progress of this "Voyage"; but it cannot propose a resolution, and merely trails off into an ellipsis.

The voice that erupts in the poem's final two lines then appears to be a dramatic response to the impasse that has preceded it. As such, it has taken even more distance from the mirroring power of the *pendu,* and arrives as a metacommentary on this voyage toward "truth." The final voice, in other words, intercedes on behalf of a voice that has been reduced to an ellipsis, to a static contradiction. In the earlier text, these lines had seemed no more than a reaffirmation of a "disgusting" identity, disguised as a halfhearted prayer. The later text's revision of the poem's finale as a dramatic space in which several voices are at play creates a far different effect. That effect is made clear in the rewriting of the earlier "gibet dégoûtant" as a "gibet symbolique": the disgusting force of the gibbet resides precisely in the possibility of reading it as a symbol, as a *correspondance* of the self in a world encountered as if it were an allegorical text. If the poem's final exclamation begs to be allowed self-contemplation without *dégoût*, then it amounts to a prayer to be freed from the power of allegory. As a metacommentary on the several voiced positions that have preceded it, these final lines call into question the value and *telos* of the strategy that has enabled the text to come into being at all.

We have observed how the later version of the "Voyage à Cythère" puts into play a set of voices, breaking the conventional unity of lyrical voice and ultimately ironizing the allegorical search for meaning in the stability of a *correspondance*. If we had limited our reading to only the later text, and had considered it a thematically self-sufficient unit, we could only find expressed there a certain impasse and frustration. Reading two versions of the poem, however, allows us to see the later version as not only expressing a wish for deallegorization, but as an enactment of that very wish. The revisions that Baudelaire worked on his earlier text have the effect of dispersing sense in order to undermine the satisfying possibility of imposing a simple allegorical reading upon "Un Voyage à Cythère." And yet, the act of undermining can be no more than a negative moment: it presupposes a structure already in place—a prototext— for its action to have any dialectical sense. The earlier version of the "Voyage" is always already in place so that its revision can come into play against it. The earlier text must be maintained as a palimpsest for the violent negativity of the revision to be brought vividly into relief.

We have also seen how Baudelaire parallels the fragmentation of the poem's voice by a careful complication of the presentation of its allegorical object—the hanged man of Cythera. The rewriting of lines 25–40 attenuates the pathos and violence in the description of the cadaver until the moment when its castration is displayed. And when we do come upon that horrific detail, we find that the pathos of a *cruel* castration has given way to the nonsense, or hypersense, of an *absolute* castration. In this peculiar hyperbole—perhaps implying an impotence beyond impotency, a powerful loss of unity, or a beautifying disfiguration—the poet has inscribed, as I see it, the fragmenting revision of his text. Whereas the earlier version traveled toward the allegorical interpretation of a vision of cruel castration, the later version spins about this central inscription of its loss of phallic unity.

Since spinning does not constitute a trajectory, readers of "Un Voyage à Cythère" have often tended, as we have seen, to put the text on the right track, orienting it by its *point de départ,* complementing it by Hugo's poem, overlooking the detail differences between versions, giving it, *in fine,* a tale. But the poem seems to have renounced a certain *charmant* quality that it attributes to the sky, and to have opted for a negative project instead. The phrase "absolument châtré" not only inscribes that project directly but echoes uncannily, at the poem's core, Cellier's cryptic remark: "beaucoup de bruit pour rien." Were one to allude to a different literary title to describe the problem of reading this text, one might say that its excessive remarking of castration constitutes a heart of darkness that will contest any enlightening unified reading. Having said this, I must at the same time disavow any attempt on my part to reduce the text to the too-innocent state of "play." There is too much density in the poem's history, too much seriousness about the way it sets out *as if* toward truth, and too much anguish in its final polylogue to allow for such trivialization. On the other hand, there is something vertiginous in the hyperbolic formulation "absolument châtré": something, indeed, almost comical. What is one to make of the role of the comical in serious works of art? That is a question that Baudelaire was trying to answer around the same time he was revising his poetry for *Les Fleurs du Mal;* let us turn to the essay that resulted from his lengthy consideration of that question, before returning to the negative poetics of "Un Voyage à Cythère."

2

The Interference of Laughter

A Certain Irrepressibility

> Si J. J. était empereur, il décréterait qu'il est
> défendu de pleurer ou de se pendre sous
> son règne, ou même de rire d'une certaine
> façon.
> *— Lettre à Jules Janin*

The revised version of "Un Voyage à Cythère" was first published on June 1, 1855, in *La Revue des deux mondes*. The text that appears in that issue of the era's leading literary journal is almost exactly the same text that we find in *Les Fleurs du Mal,* with one major exception: lines 33 through 36 were genteelly replaced by a modest line of dots. The expurgation thus spared the journal's public from confronting the unseemly—in fact, hyperbolic—violence of "absolute castration." The good intentions of the editors in effecting this cultural repression were not entirely satisfied, however. One month later the scene resurfaced in *De l'Essence du rire,* reinscribed prosaically, in a context of hyperbole, vertigo, and violence, as an example of what Baudelaire was trying to define as "le comique absolu." The repressed, as it were, returned in disguise—a different journal, a different genre—but no less resonant.

The reinscription that I am talking about occurs near the end of the essay, as Baudelaire recalls an evening spent watching some English actors perform their version of Guignol farce. The memory of that evening is particularly vivid because the English interpretation of Guignol, like the final version of "Un Voyage à Cythère," was an act of violent rewriting: "Il m'a semblé que le signe distinctif de ce genre comique était la violence. . . . Quant au moral, le fond était le même que celui du Pierrot que tout le monde connaît. . . . Seulement, là où Deburau eût trempé le bout du doigt pour le lécher, [le Pierrot anglais] y plongeait les deux poings et les deux pieds."[1] From Pierrot's facial grimaces to his movements on stage, from his excessive thievery to his rather blunt expression of desire, this English interpretation of him violates even the most minimal standards of *bienséance*: "c'était le vertige de l'hyperbole" (539).

To demonstrate the "terrible et irrésistible" force of the hyperbolic performance, Baudelaire recounts the ubiquitous moment of Guignol justice, when Pierrot is brutally punished for his misdeeds. Strangely enough, Pierrot's fate on that night was to be guillotined: "Pourquoi le guillotine au lieu de la pendaison, en pays anglais? . . . Je l'ignore; sans doute pour amener ce qu'on va voir" (539). What we come to see is a frightful beheading, described in fulsome detail so that the joke that follows it can better be appreciated; after the beheading, the inveterate thief Pierrot manages to steal back his own severed head: "Mais voilà que, subitement, le torse raccourci, mû par la monomanie irrésistible du vol, se dressait, escamotait victorieusement sa propre tête comme un jambon ou une bouteille de vin, et, bien plus avisé que le grand saint Denis, la fourrait dans sa poche!" (539). Baudelaire's demonstration of *le comique absolu* thus culminates in a fantastic scene in which an event of castration is reappropriated by the victim. As soon as this joke is told, the subject shifts from Pierrot to writing: "Avec une plume tout cela est pâle et glacé. Comment la plume pourrait-elle rivaliser avec la pantomime?" (540). Writing, then, tends to be "pale" in the same way that the usual—French—rendition of Pierrot has him "pâle comme la lune" (538). In contrast to the pallor both of writing and of his French precursor, the English Pierrot appears truly larger than life, in spite of a certain lack of stature:

> C'était un homme court et gros, ayant augmenté sa prestance par un costume chargé de rubans, qui faisaient autour de sa jubilante personne l'office des plumes et du duvet autour des oiseaux, ou de la fourrure autour des angoras. (538)

The movement from "rubans" to "plumes" and then to cats is a particularly resonant one. Pierrot's beribboned costume must lend him, in his wild gyrations upon the stage, the air of a living thyrsus; and the thyrsus, as we know from the prose poem "Le Thyrse," is that jubilant object that figures for Baudelaire the very figurality of writing. In the prose poem, "le poète des chats"—as he calls himself elsewhere—employs the figure of the thyrsus to set into motion a meditation on the spinning trajectories of metaphor.[2] In the passage cited above, the thyrsuslike aspect of Pierrot may associate him with some mode of writing—a writing that undergoes and then recuperates its own dismemberment. There is no doubt that Pierrot is seen as *absolutely* comical, nor that the absolute nature of his hyperbolic performance challenges the mimetic power of the essay's discourse. It is too soon to decide whether the passage performs, instead of evoking, its version of *le comique absolu,* but we can suspect that the pale *plume* of the pen and the *plumes* of Pierrot's costume have both to do with writing. That is, Baudelaire writes out his admiration for a joke that is built around a performance of absolute castration, and in doing so he not only reinscribes the expurgated scene of the "Voyage," but mobilizes the problem of a writing that might operate in a way comparable to the vertiginous English Pierrot. But it remains to be seen how the notion of the *absolu* functions in this essay. Further, we need to explore the extent to which the topic of writing is motivated earlier in the text.

The Intervention of Pure Poetry

> Fancioulle me prouvait, d'une manière
> péremptoire, irréfutable, que l'ivresse de
> l'Art est plus apte que toute autre à voiler
> les terreurs du gouffre. . . .
> – *Une Mort héroïque*

There is a moment in his discussion of laughter when Baudelaire seems to swerve off the course of his until-then-carefully-structured argument to address, obliquely but intriguingly, the subject of poetry:

> . . . et, enfin, [nous voyons] que si dans ces mêmes nations ultracivilisées, une intelligence, poussée par une ambition supérieure, veut franchir les limites de l'orgeuil mondain et s'élancer hardiment vers la poésie pure, dans cette poésie, limpide et profonde comme la nature, le rire fera défaut comme dans l'âme du Sage. (532–33)

Let us situate this remark within the essay before commenting on it, not only to get a sense of its context, but to judge better how it occurs suddenly, without thematic preparation, as an excessive production.

The essay on laughter is divided into six parts: an introduction that explains the occasion for writing, four short chapters on the psychology of laughter, and a longer final part devoted to various manifestations of the comical in literature and art. The remark on "pure poetry" occurs at the end of the first of two long paragraphs that make up part 4 of the essay. That first paragraph opens by announcing that the essay's argument on the psychology of laughter will now be reiterated:

> Maintenant, résumons un peu, et établissons plus visiblement les propositions principales, qui sont comme une espèce de théorie du rire. (532)

As he recapitulates the theory, Baudelaire calls upon the Pascalian model of the two infinities to evoke the median psychological space from which laughter must emanate. The reference to Pascal is not acknowledged, but is a virtual citation:

> [Le rire] est essentiellement contradictoire, c'est-à-dire qu'il est à la fois signe d'une grandeur infinie et d'une misère infinie, misère infinie relativement à l'Etre absolu dont il possède la conception, grandeur infinie relativement aux animaux. C'est du choc perpétuel de ces deux infinis que se dégage le rire. (532)

As the summation continues, we find working in it not only the iconography of Pascal, but a Pascalian logic as well: laughter operates in the essay as a kind of hinge between the two faculties of mind that Pascal called "imagination" and "reason." In Pascal, imagination is at the service of metaphysical bad faith, while reason allows man the apperception of his true condition:

> [L'imagination] ne peut rendre sages les fous; mais elle les rend heureux, à l'envi de la raison, qui ne peut rendre ses amis que misérable, l'une les couvrant de gloire, l'autre de honte.[3]

For Baudelaire, laughter explodes from man as he intuits his superiority to the Other, and with that laughter arises an "idea of superiority." That idea, however, operates like Pascal's "reason" to enable the laughing man to conceive of his own inferiority relative to the concepts which the idea of superiority can bring to mind: unbounded superiority, infinite grandeur, and absolute Being. Laughter reminds the laughing man that his momentary intuition of superiority is already grounded in a certain fallenness. Thus laughter can always lend itself to *dédoublement*, just as that self-reflexivity can generate an ironic laughter: the exemplary laughter of Melmoth, whom Baudelaire discusses in part 3, is both triumphant and deflationary. On the other hand, the man totally possessed of Pascalian right reason would not ever find himself laughing: "Le rire," Baudelaire continues, "est signe d'infériorité relativement aux sages, qui par l'innocence contemplative de leur esprit se rapprochent de l'enfance."

The paragraph then begins to close by re-citing the two figures from literature whom Baudelaire had deployed to create an archaeology of laughter. The Romantically beatific Virginie, from *Paul et Virginie*, had emblematized the innocent savage who could only be confounded by the humor of modern Europe. And Melmoth had served afterwards as the prototype of the modern sardonic consciousness. The sentence that reminds the reader of how these two intertextual figures functioned in the essay could well end at this point; the summation has been completed by the discussion of Melmoth. Instead, the sentence pushes on past a semicolon to remark on the laughterless quality of a hypothetical "pure poetry." It has not been a question of poetry at any preceding moment of the essay, nor will poetry be mentioned in it again. How are we to read this excessively singular instance where the relation between the comical and the purely poetic is *almost* explored?

First, we might note that, although the remark does not constitute a transition, it occurs at a transition, since the essay will now abandon its discussion of the psychology of laughter to pursue a discussion of the nature of comical scenes. The remark is thus not only out of place in the paragraph of summation, it is also without any place within the essay as such: it has fallen in the gap between two different moments of the argument. If it is without a place

within the text, it then asks to be read as a misplaced remark—
perhaps as the essay's fallen epigraph.

If we lend the remark on "pure poetry" the kind of liminal authority of an epigraph, we must stress that it seems to lean, in its
invocation of purity, on the Kantian notion of the "fine" quality of
the Fine Arts, or *schöne Kunst*. Fine Art in the *Critique of Judgment* is
no more self-evident a concept than "pure poetry" is in the essay on
laughter, but the prediction that such poetry will be "limpid and
profound like nature" can be aligned with the title of paragraph 45
of the *Critique*: "Beautiful art is an art in so far as it seems like nature." In that paragraph, Kant writes:

> In a product of the Fine Arts, we must become conscious that
> it is art and not nature; but yet the purposiveness in its form
> must seem to be as free from all constraint [*Zwang,* also "com-
> pulsion"] of arbitrary rules as if it were a product of pure na-
> ture. On this feeling of freedom in the play of our cognitive
> faculties, which must at the same time be purposive, rests that
> pleasure [*Lust,* as distinguished from *Genuss,* "enjoyment"]
> which alone is universally communicable, without being based
> on concepts.[4]

The political, economic, and rhetorical implications of this passage
can be, and have been, explored at length.[5] For the moment and purpose at hand, we need first to gloss it in the most rudimentary way.
Fine Art, says Kant, must be recognizable as art; that is, it must not
let itself be confused with the mere activity of nature, or with natural activity. It needs a frame of a sort set about it to distinguish it as
an eminently human pursuit—as distinct, for example, from the
nesting of bees, whose creation stems only from instinct. If art *seems*
free from constraint, it is because, as Kant says elsewhere, it does
not follow mechanical rules for iterative imitation.[6] Being a product
dependent on the free will and talent—or genius—of the artist, it
assumes an aura of originality; that is, rather than follow the rules
by which art can imitate other art or the objects of nature, Fine Art
is in tune with a higher set of rules: those rules by which nature

produces freely the phenomenal world with its aspect of "purposiveness" while without disclosing its purpose. Fine Art does not imitate the objects of nature, but rather the process of nature, the *natura naturans,* which generates those very objects. At the same time it is constrained by its formality so that it is distinct and distinguishable from nature, with the result that it gives rise to a certain pleasure in its beholder. That pleasure (*Lust*) is not derived from the concepts of science, nor dependent on the enjoyment of gratification (*Genuss*) of the senses; being thus delivered from both the idealism of conceptual knowledge and the opacity of the personal experience of the body, it is available to universal appreciation of its Fine-Artfulness. In Baudelaire's terms, the purity of "pure poetry" consists in its springlike welling up and pellucid flowing forth (*limpide* derives from the Latin *lympha,* "water, esp. clear river or spring water"); in its transparency and yet its inscrutable depth. It is like nature by virtue of the immediate generosity of its production—its sourcefulness—and of its mystery, its depth, its veiled purpose. The writer of such poetry is the writer blessed with what Kant calls "genius": the gift of translating freely into Art the world's gift of giving.

But Baudelaire does not speak of poetic genius in his remark on pure poetry. Rather, it is a question of high ambition, of surpassing pride, and of headlong pursuit. The project of pure poetry seems tinged, from the essay's point of view, with the shadow of hubris. Further, his remark has the syntactic form of a conditional sentence: "si . . . une intelligence . . . veut . . . ." Now the conditions of this sentence do not lie outside the realm of possibility, as they would if the present indicative "veut" were cast in the imperfect, but his formulation is at best tentative nonetheless. Hugo, by contrast, spoke with great assurance about genius in his "Préface de Cromwell," and showed no tentativeness in such distant but faithful paraphrases of Kant as:

> Il n'y a ni règles, ni modèles, ou plutôt il n'y a d'autres règles que les lois générales de la nature qui planent sur l'art tout entier, et les lois spéciales qui, pour chaque composition, résultent des conditions d'existence propres à chaque sujet.[7]

Compared to the full-blown theories of genius whose terms it appropriates, Baudelaire's liminal remark is teasingly ambiguous—a sort of *invitation à la lecture*. If somebody achieves a "poésie pure," it says, then that writing will be devoid of laughter's contamination. To invert the terms of that proposition, we are drawn to conclude that a poetry less than "pure" must always entail, in some way, the element of comicality. To discover what the work of such an element within poetry might be, we need to read further in the essay on laughter, focusing on the section where Baudelaire proposes *le comique absolu* in contradistinction to a lesser type of the comical, which he relegates to the classification of the merely *significatif.*

Comicality and Signification

> C'est que l'essence de la poésie de
> Baudelaire est d'opérer, au prix d'une
> tension anxieuse, la fusion avec le sujet
> (l'immanence) de ces objets, *qui se perdent* à
> la fois pour causer l'angoisse et la réfléchir.
> –Georges Bataille, *La Littérature et le mal*

Like Freud in *Jokes and Their Relation to the Unconscious,* Baudelaire was struck by the suddenness of the laughter provoked by certain comical objects. Freud writes: "A nontendentious joke scarcely ever achieves the sudden burst of laughter which makes tendentious ones so irresistible."[8] He then reads that suddenness as symptomatic of the fact that the tendentious joke can have only two purposes: "It is either a *hostile* joke (serving the purpose of aggressiveness, satire, or defense) or an *obscene* joke (serving the purpose of exposure)." The intensely sudden laugh testifies to the joke's power to satisfy lustful or hostile instincts despite social and psychic censure.[9] Baudelaire, on the other hand, did not investigate the sudden laugh as the symptom of a psychic process, but instead used the phenomenon of suddenness as the key to a typology of the comical based on temporality. In part 5 of *De l'Essence du rire,* he formulates his distinction between the "comique absolu" and the "comique significatif." The *absolutely* comical, he writes, elicits not merely laughter of any sort but rather:

> le rire subit; en face du comique significatif, il n'est pas défendu
> de rire après coup; cela n'arguë pas contre sa valeur; c'est une
> question de rapidité d'analyse. (536)

In other words, the comical called "significant" (Baudelaire never
explains or justifies his choice of that adjective) entails deferral in
its comprehension; its comical meaning never coincides with the
gesture that produces it. With the absolutely comical, though, the
sense of the laughter having been produced is erased, and laughter,
described as "a nervous convulsion, an involuntary spasm like a
sneeze" (530), simply comes, all at once. The notion of the absolutely comical seems to establish a pole of immediacy, a temporal
experience where event and meaning completely coincide. From
that pole of immediacy a time line might be drawn, to show the
space of deferral in which the signification of the significantly comical takes place. To put it differently, one could represent the absolutely comical by drawing a single geometric point, "a," to show
immediacy, and then two points, "b" and "b'" connected by a line,
to show the deferral of the significantly comical. The deferral of the
second type of comical event makes it difficult to speak of a comical
event at all, for the "event" becomes multiple in the play of object,
signification, and comprehension. Freud has a similar problem distinguishing between the effectiveness of technique and that of cen-
sured purpose in tendentious jokes. "Thus," he observes, "strictly
speaking, we do not know what we are laughing at" (102).

But if Baudelaire, as cited above, seems to propose a two-part
model for our experience of the comical, and to rely on a mutually
exclusive opposition between immediacy and deferral for his discussion, he nevertheless ends part 5 of the essay by complicating, after
the fact, all that has gone before.

> J'ai dit: comique absolu; il faut toutefois prendre garde. Au
> point de vue définitif, il n'y a plus que la joie. Le comique ne
> peut être absolu que relativement à l'humanité déchue, et c'est
> ainsi que je l'entends. (536)

The term "absolute," then, is only a relative one: all the comical,
absolute and significant, must be subsumed under the category of

fallen experience. Opposed to fallenness is innocence—the harm-less state of joy. Baudelaire had already invited us on an excursion to that state, in less theoretical and more sardonic terms:

> Le rire des enfants est comme un épanouissement de fleur. C'est la joie de recevoir, la joie de respirer, la joie de s'ouvrir, la joie de contempler, de vivre, de grandir. C'est une joie de plante. (534)

Here is a myth of childhood that is immediately revealed to be no more than mystification: we are told in the next sentence that chil-dren are no more than "little men, that is to say, budding Satans." Within the myth, in the depiction of the state of joy, the attitude toward "joy" is clearly ironic: the second sentence uses anaphora and ellipsis to accelerate in a crescendo of passive, nice occupations, only to be sharply undermined by the terse final sentence. At the extreme, the pole of immediacy, we find ensconced in the land of joy only a verdant homunculus—a sort of "sanctified vegetable," to borrow the well-known phrase from one of Baudelaire's letters.[10] This mythic joy no doubt resembles the limpid pleasure of Kantian *Lust* far more than it does *Genuss,* that enjoyment which involves the mediation of the body. "La joie" is, in fact, represented as so happy, so immediate a state that the signal power of laughter to split the face fades into the mute serenity of a smile:

> Aussi, généralement, [le rire des enfants] est-ce plutôt le sourire, quelque chose d'analogue au balancement de queue des chiens ou au ronron des chats. (534)

The charming, joyous face is as unified as the sea that torments a certain Cytherian tourist.

What is the effect of this excursion into the land of joy, and of its belated theoretical elaboration at the end of part 5? "Joy" designates a nonhuman limit-concept where the sound of the voice erupting in laughter would never be heard. Conversely, whenever laughter oc-curs, it signals the absence of joy, the fallenness of human being, and the installation of signification by deferral. For the discussion of joy shifts the other terms of the argument: since the comical is always within the fallen, it is never absolute in the immediate sense, and always significant, always deferred—significant because of its situation in a structure of deferral. The state of joy is smilingly silent; the state of laughter is noisily significant. As we have seen above, the laughter elicited by the "comique absolu" is sudden, appearing to be immediate: but that immediacy is only apparent, for the true immediacy of self-presence precludes laughter. The two modes of the comical cannot be set into a relation of mutually exclusive disjunction. They do not exist in an oppositional stance of either-or, but rather in an economic relation of more or less. Thinking "joy" reveals that all of the comical is marked by the structure of deferral, to a greater or lesser extent.

All of the comical, then, is inscribed within fallenness, which subjects it to some degree of deferral, some temporal gap between subject and sense. If Baudelaire's use of the adjective "significant" at first seemed an arbitrary choice for marking that deferral, it must begin to be read as highly resonant—as if the essay on laughter were a blind, behind which an exploration of the temporality of signification were taking place. That conjecture feels less far-reaching when we look back to the analogy implicit in the following remark, which is made while the opposition between "absolute" and "significant" *seems* to be firmly in place:

> Il est évident qu'il faut distinguer, et qu'il y a là un degré de plus. Le comique [significatif] est, au point de vue artistique, une imitation, [le comique absolu], une création. (535)

The move to the "artistic point of view," like the epigraphical remark on pure poetry, is made possible by invoking Kantian esthetics. By aligning the absolute with the post-Kantian, Romantic notion of creativity, the essay implies that the objects called "absolutely comical" are like the poetry of genius—springing forth with unmediated vigor from the unique imagination of the creator-artist who can boast, like Hernani, "Je suis une force qui va."[11] On the other hand, the notion of the "significant comical" is also shifted by this move to the level of esthetics; the temporal deferral characteristic of the *significatif* is thus linked to, and perhaps explained by, the imitative, derived, nonoriginal, intertextual mode of its production. And where the *absolu* had at first seemed to participate in the immediacy that would also characterize a limpid *poésie pure,* we now find the essay undermining the possibility of clearly opposing the two categories of the comical. Insofar as the "absolute" comes to share irremediably in the deferral of the "significant," and insofar as we are led to consider the categories from an "artistic point of view," the meditation on laughter can be said to call into question the ideology of artistic creativity. That is, the essay on laughter confronts the gap between self and self-presence, because it is that joyless gap that laughter always signals; in that confrontation, the opposition of "absolute" and "significant" begins to erode, while that of "creation" and "imitation" follows the same path. What Baudelaire has singled out in the phenomenon of laughter as its most telling trait is the testimony it bears to the deferral of presence, a deferral that leads to the mediation of significant codes, that enables representation and denotation, and that imbeds meaning in a temporally complex structure. The comical is *always* significant in that it never simply, joyfully coincides with itself, never constitutes a simple event, but rather arises from its dispersal in the structure of the *après coup.* Thinking the problem of this significance leads the essay toward a questioning of the notion of original creativity, at which point the comical—always significant, always derived, always deferred, more or less—begins to sound like a latent representative of writing.

Having said this, let me recall briefly an early passage in the essay, in which Baudelaire tries to define and restrict the artistic objects that will concern him in his discussion of laughter. The genre of caricature interests him especially at this point, but it is not a question of all types of caricature. One type is merely topical and journalistic. Limited as it is to the specificity of an historical situation against which it derives its comical effect, this type is prone to evanescence and replacement: "Comme les feuilles volantes du journalisme, elles disparaissent emportées par le souffle incessant qui en amène de nouvelles . . ." (525). These topical caricatures, because of their *mere* topicality, do not interest him. There exist others, however, that resist the evanescent referentiality of the first type; indeed, they have been inoculated against such evanescence, by a certain infusion: "[elles] contiennent un élément mystérieux, durable, éternel, qui les recommande à l'attention des artistes" (526). This mysterious element that elevates so low a genre as caricature to an artifact worthy of artistic appreciation is called simply "beauty":

> Chose curieuse et vraiment digne d'attention que l'introduc-tion de cet élément insaisissable du beau jusque dans les oeuvres destinées à représenter à l'homme sa propre laideur morale et physique! Et, chose non moins mystérieuse, ce spec-tacle lamentable excite en lui une hilarité immortelle et incor-rigible. Voilà donc le véritable sujet et cet article. (526)

Most striking here is the way "beauty"—the element that weighs down, anchors, and protects the work against the winds of change—is portrayed as an aftereffect. Beauty is added on to ugliness, de-forming mere reprehensibility into a durable, *beautiful* sin. Beauty is not constitutive in the caricature, but rather comes after the fact, to make the distasteful taste even worse—and thereby granting it du-ration. The combination of the beautiful and the ugly does not re-sult in some sort of mean between the two, but instead in a super-ugly and a funny-ugly, which has the power to resist a reduction to the merely topical. The hilarity of the spectator is of a special kind, and testifies to the resistance of the comical object to simple re-cuperation. Beauty short-circuits the sentimental and moral re-sponse, which would reduce the text to mere exemplum, and raises that text to the level of the fascinating. An elusive and resistant ele-ment of mysterious force is superimposed upon a representation of human decrepitude, and the injection of this resistant beauty into a moral platitude results in an equally complex response from the spectator. This added-on element, this inoculation against recupera-tion, although it is brought up in relation to caricature, sounds like the process of rewriting that results in "Un Voyage à Cythère." The rewriting of that text certainly problematizes the recourse to make total sense of the text through allegorical and moral reduction. Ought, then, the revision and decomposition of the scene of the *pendu* give rise to an appropriate hilarity? Has the rewriting of that text infused it with a durable comicality akin to that found in certain caricatures? If so, then the "Voyage" would establish itself as the antithesis to a *poésie pure* of limpid, silent seriousness. And we might well ask of the passage cited above: what, then, *is* the veritable subject of the essay on laughter? If beauty can be, among other things, the inscription of a hard humor within a text, preserving that text from moralistic consumption, granting it a fascinating resistance, then we might propose that the veritable subject of the essay is that which tends toward the indelible, toward the irrecuperable—in short, the subject of writing.

It is not surprising, then, to find Baudelaire beginning his essay with the confession that he is writing out an obsession:

> Je ne veux pas écrire un traité de la caricature; je veux simple-
> ment faire part au lecteur de quelques réflexions qui me sont
> venues souvent au sujet de ce genre singulier. Ces réflexions
> étaient devenues pour moi une espèce d'obsession; j'ai voulu
> me soulager. (525)

The essay opens by announcing that its writing is a therapeutic per-formance—a writing out of several virulent "réflexions." As the prolegomenon finishes, and the argument begins in part 2, we find the confession repeated, with the difference that these "réflexions" are now evoked as deriving from a textual rather than a purely sub-jective source:

> *Le Sage ne rit qu'en tremblant.* De quelles lèvres pleines d'auto-
> rité, de quelle plume parfaitement orthodoxe est tombée cette
> étrange et saisissante maxime? Nous vient-elle du roi phi-
> losophe de la Judée? Faut-il l'attribuer à Joseph de Maistre, ce
> soldat animé de l'Esprit-Saint? J'ai un vague souvenir de l'avoir
> lue dans un de ses livres, mais donnée comme citation, sans
> doute. Cette sévérité de pensée et de style va bien à la sainteté
> majestueuse de Bossuet; mais la tournure elliptique de la pensée
> et la finesse quintessenciée me porteraient plutôt à en attribuer
> l'honneur à Bourdaloue, l'impitoyable psychologue chrétien.
> Cette singulière maxime me revient sans cesse à l'esprit depuis
> que j'ai conçu le projet de cet article, et j'ai voulu m'en débar-
> rasser tout d'abord. (526–27)

The reflections which had often "come to me" have here become the ceaseless "returning to mind" of another text. And no sooner is the specifically textual nature of the "reflection" revealed than the essay engages the reader in a wild-goose chase for the "source" of that other text—a chase during which it is proposed that one possible source was only the site of a citation that is here being repeated. It is in this curious array of repeated confessions, obsessive reflections, elusive sources, and the endless return of a "singular phrase" that the essay has its beginning. Can that beginning be located and localized, or does it resemble the multiple event of the significantly comical? That is the question posed by the questioning of the reader in the above passage—we are asked, in effect, to try to name the beginning of the essay. The questioning engages us in the structure of the significantly comical, and were we to answer that the essay has its beginning in Bossuet—the acknowledged source of the "singular phrase"—we would be missing the joke. The name of "Bossuet," and the linear historical attitude the utterance of it would imply, can in no way stabilize or account for the ceaseless returning of the phrase to the mind of the writer, nor fill the abyss of the repetitive confession of that obsessive repetition at the essay's beginning. The "singular phrase" stands out by its ability to multiply and fragment itself—by its demand to be unpacked and translated into an essay. The joke of the essay's beginning lies in its demonstration that its beginning has always begun somewhere else, through the mediation of other texts.

This joke exists at the expense of certain Kantian expectations. Like the remark on pure poetry and the invoking of pure creativity, it leans on Kant in order to derive its context, but finishes by leaning hard enough to deform, if not displace, its frame. As the essay on laughter repetitively calls into question the notion of its origin, as it produces itself amid obsessions and intertexts, it demonstrates a writing that is radically different from the naturelike emanation theorized in Kantian esthetics. Where Kant prescribes that Fine Art appear free from constraint or compulsion (*Zwang*), here the essay begins by confessing an obsession. And where Kantian theory dictates a writing that is "limpid and profound like nature" in its free creativity, here the essay begins by nervously unburdening itself of an obsessive maxim from the huge public domain of other writing.

The joke is in the fallen mode of the significantly comical, of course; it is at the same time a kind of metajoke, dramatizing the structure of deferral within the writing process of this meditation on deferral. The joke, however, is limited in its import by its very nature: it can testify to some form of aggressivity or to a desire to expose—as Freud told us—but it is always a sublimated performance. Merely leaning on a few received ideas concerning Romantic writing does not begin to offer a countervailing theory of textual productivity. The essay's funny beginning may assign a similar ontology to both the written and the comical, but we must look elsewhere for a less rapid elaboration of that problem.

"Here": The Arena of Difference

> Lorsque aucune langue connue n'est à votre
> disposition, il faut bien se résoudre à *voler*
> *un langage*—comme on volait autrefois un
> pain.
> — *Roland Barthes par Roland Barthes*

Such an elaboration occurs one page later, when a "poetical sup-position" introduces the "figure" of Virginie into the "here" of modern Paris, apparently wresting her from her happy home in the novel *Paul et Virginie,* by Rousseau's friend and disciple Bernardin de Saint-Pierre. Let us take this figure, as Baudelaire suggests, and follow the circuit of its configuration. In this section, we will examine the essay's creation of a Fall for Virginie; next we will consider its prophecy of a kind of redemption that will be achieved as an apprenticeship to laughter. In both sections, I want to insist on the larcenous mode of Baudelaire's writing: he is obviously stealing a "character" from someone else's book to talk about laughter, and he is also "stealing a language," as Barthes says—an act of prolepsis in this case, since the object of the second theft was a language that had not yet come into conscious existence at the time.

Virginie is invited into the essay because "[elle] symbolise par-faitement la pureté et la naïveté absolues" (528). She arrives on the scene:

> Elle tombe ici en pleine civilisation turbulente, débordante et
> méphitique, elle, toute imprégnée des pures et riches senteurs
> de l'Inde; elle se rattache à l'humanité par la famille et par
> l'amour, par sa mère et par son amant, son Paul, angélique
> comme elle, et dont le sexe ne se distingue pour ainsi dire pas
> du sien dans les ardeurs inassouvies d'un amour qui s'ignore.
> (528–29)

This delicate evocation of Virginie's naiveté focuses on two points;
she does not yet know, or she has un-known, the fact of sexual difference, and, concomitantly, her "family" consists solely of the
mother. This state of unisexed simplicity makes her vulnerable, on
the level of psychological characterization, to the events which will
soon befall her. But on the other hand, Virginie begins, in the essay,
in a position parallel to that of the essay's beginning—neither she
nor it can know where they come from. As she arrives on the scene
of writing, "here," Virginie seems to repeat in mythic form the earlier questioning of sources with which the essay's rhetoric had engaged the reader.

But if Virginie does not know where she comes from, she has
been invited, or rather coerced, upon the scene to dramatize something of that discovery. The fallen world into which she falls—
modern Paris—is a world overlayered with an overabundance of
sense; "en pleine civilisation turbulente, débordante et méphitique."
In this "here" she happens upon a caricatural drawing, and in particular a lewd satire of the lascivious goings-on at the court of Louis
XVI: "un Gavarni de ce temps-là et des meilleurs." She perceives an
image whose very impact derives from the peculiar layering of its
meaning:

> La caricature est double: le dessin et l'idée: le dessin violent,
> l'idée mordante et voilée; complication d'éléments pénibles
> pour un esprit naïf. . . . (529)

Virginie has been violated by a certain violence, and bitten through
a veil.

Baudelaire writes simply that she beholds the unknown, but follows the apparent simplicity of that statement in typical fashion, by complicating it:

> Du reste, elle ne comprend guère ni ce que cela veut dire ni à quoi cela sert. Et pourtant, voyez-vous ce reploiement d'ailes subit, ce frémissement d'une âme qui se voile et veut se retirer? L'ange a senti que le scandale était là. (529)

The sudden folding of her wings shows that Virginie knows what she does not know that she knows: she may not have the answer to the childlike question of what certain things are for, but she senses with the suddenness of the *comique absolu* that she has fallen into a world where meanings are somehow already in place before they are come upon. In other words, the duplicity of the caricature by which she is confronted initiates Virginie not only into the world of sexual difference, but into the temporal structure characteristic of human sexuality—the *nachträglich* structure where meanings are prepared in advance only to appear later, often in displacement.[12] The significantly comical display of sexual difference occasions a "complication of painful elements" for this "absolutely naive" spirit who would apprehend meaning transparently, all at once: *d'un coup* rather than *après coup*. "Here," meaning arrives beneath a veil, bitingly, cutting off this falling angel from her sense of the fullness of the present, from her sense of the present as a meaningful moment. The veiled joke of the caricature resides neither in the drawing nor in its beholder, but instead in a third place that enables the drawing to be significant. The place from which the joke of the duplicitous caricature is available functions similarly to the Lacanian notion of the "place of the Other," where a collection of signifiers lies already constituted prior to any significant exchange between subjects.[13] We may read the "scandal" that Virginie senses as an intuitive understanding that her subjectivity, her potential to signify and be signifiable, is constituted from that other place beyond her grasp.

Virginie comes into the "here" of Baudelaire's essay, then, to "discover" her "castration." By this I do not mean to immure her in the imaginary play of the "phallic phase" of child development psychology; I do not want to restrict the scene to the discovery of a genitality that is wrongly interpreted as a mutilation or a lack. In the first place, Virginie is not a little girl, but a sign from another text. Further, she has been brought from that text to play a role in an essay that writes out an obsession with laughter as if the subject of laughter were an avatar for the subject of writing.

Since it is a question of signification and deferral, the parable of Virginie's "castration" lends itself to a reading through the optic of Lacan, where Freudian theory is conjoined with aspects of a linguistic theory that postdates it. And if we turn to a Lacanian instead of Lacan, it is because Julia Kristeva has formulated the most concise reading of him that can illuminate our reading at this point. At stake in her discussion is the drawing of a parallel between two pairs of terms. The first pair consists of the components of the Saussurian sign: the signified and the signifier. The second pair comprises the "self" as an isolated unity perceived in a moment of identification with a mirror image, on the one hand, and the mobile, unbound energy of the body and its drives, as represented in the unconscious, on the other. The cutting edge of "castration" will be to stress the irreducible gap that inheres between the terms of each pair. The breach between signified and signifier, represented by the bar that separates them, is inherent in their unmotivated relation to each other in a system where signification is a product of difference between signifiers, rather than of the existence of positive terms for those signifiers. And the imago-self is irretrievably alienated from the living body it comes to represent, being always an image of the self that returns to the self from a mirroring other. Kristeva's discussion of castration begins with a familiar developmental fiction, but moves rapidly toward an ontology of signification:

> Addressee of every demand, the mother occupies the place of alterity: her full body, the receptacle and guarantor of the demands, stands for all the narcissistic—and therefore imaginary—satisfactions; which is to say that she is the phallus. The discovery of castration detaches the subject from its dependency in relation to the mother and, through this lack, makes the phallic function a symbolic function—*the* symbolic function. A decisive moment of great consequence: finding its

identity in the symbolic register, the subject is *separated* from its implication in the mother, localizes its pleasure (*jouissance*) as genital and transfers the motility of the semiotic into the order of the symbolic [to become signifiers].[14]

"Castration," while retaining all the fantasmatic intensity that it enjoys in the writing of Freud, becomes an explanatory metaphor for the conditions imposed on the subject in order for it to enter actively into language. As such a metaphor, it stresses being cut off from the body of the mother (a "moment" already prepared by the mirror stage, when the infant is captivated by a unified representation of the disparate sensations that had, until then, amounted to its only perception of its body), as the basic precondition for the access to language. That is, the infant must see itself as a separated and separate object, identifiable and thus signifiable, in order to assume a position in signification—as a name, a gender, or a pronoun, for instance. To follow Lacan more closely than does Kristeva at this point, the narcissistic phantasy of the infant, the imaginary construction that castration comes to disrupt, consists in being the mother's phallus—the sole object of her desire—and "castration" marks the necessary abandonment of that phantasy as the infant, etymologically "he who is incapable of speech," moves toward language. The general drift of the link between castration and language is summarized by Serge Leclaire, who writes that castration is "fundamentally" tied to language:

> Access to language implies something of castration—a renouncing of a primal narcissistic image, or, better yet, a renouncing of the first words that support the representation that parents have of us. Castration—sexual determination—is a way of access to language, to speech.[15]

Just as sexual determination signals the renunciation of a closed and polymorphous autoeroticism, castration marks the end of an imaginary plenitude in and through the mother. These constitutive events exact a certain price: a loss-to-language. That is, the subject identifies its "self" as that isolated entity which can be represented in the register of the signifier, as "boy," "John," "he," "I," and so on. And this identification of the self with the nameable ego-imago causes anything that exceeds or subverts that representation to become the object of censure. Furthermore, the subject enters into this process of signification only by submitting to a variety of codes which both predate and delimit its subjective position in them. Thus Kristeva goes on to say:

> the gap (*béance*) between the ego-imago and the motility of drives . . . is the cutting off (*coupure*) that establishes what Lacan calls the place of the Other as the place of the "signifier." The subject is prevented from appearing there "by an always purer signifier," but this failure-to-be-there grants an other the role of making signification possible; and this other, who is no longer the mother (from whom the separation is accomplished by the mirror stage and castration), is given as the place of the signifier that Lacan calls the Other. . . . It is a matter of dependency in relation to the mother, cut off in order to be transformed into a symbolic relation with others; the constitution of the Other is indispensable for communication with others. With the result that the cutting off of signifiers from signifieds is synonymous with social sanction; it is "the first censure of the social order" [citing Lacan].[16]

In Baudelaire's essay on laughter, the joke that is in place before Virginie finds it comes to her from the place of the Other—a social reservoir of meaning. Thus her entry into the realm of the comical parallels the entry of the infant into signification. This initiation into the comical world is accomplished by a "biting" caricature that leaves Virginie's present in bits. Her experience of the lewd caricature's duplicitous textuality gives rise to an affect that is described. but not named:

> Et, en vérité, je vous le dis, qu'elle ait compris ou qu'elle n'ait pas compris, il lui restera de cette impression je ne sais quel malaise, quelque chose qui ressemble à la peur. (529)[17]

As Virginie beholds the unknown—or the unassimilable—she feels something akin to fear that is not quite fear itself. Faced with the unknown, she does not feel fear, because fear requires a specifiable object, as both Heidegger and Freud have shown; the *malaise* "that resembles fear" is called anxiety, a word that "describes," Freud writes, "a particular state of expecting the danger or preparing for it, even though it may be an unknown one."[18] Fear is the result of perceiving a clear and present danger, while anxiety is elicited by the sense that the future holds within it some danger not yet disclosed. Virginie's fall into the "here" of the essay occasions the signal of anxiety.

What is to be made of this fall into anxiety? In his late essay on inhibition, symptom, and anxiety, Freud attempts to track anxiety back into infantile life and, so doing, reveals its peculiar structure. Writing against the Rankian notion that anxiety has its origin in the "birth trauma," Freud shows that the flood of stimuli accompanying the emergence of the fetus into the world cannot, *d'un coup*, constitute anxiety:

> In the act of birth there is an objective danger to the preservation of life; we know what that means in the reality sense. But psychologically it has no meaning at all. The danger attending birth still has no psychic content. For certainly we cannot imagine as existing in the fetus anything which in the least approaches any sort of knowledge of the possibility of death as an outcome.[19]

That is, anxiety is a response to a situation where a potential danger is felt to threaten, which presupposes a psychological capacity to recognize danger as dangerous. It is logically impossible to admit such a capacity at the moment of birth, although that moment may come to serve as the prototype of the danger situation. "It is easy to say," Freud continues, "that the newborn infant will repeat the affect of anxiety in every situation which reminds it of the birth situation. The real question, however, is by what and of what it is reminded" (74). The real question becomes one of explaining the recognition of danger.

Danger is first perceived by the infant as an economic disturbance, as "an increase of tension arising from the nongratification of its needs—a situation against which it is powerless." If birth can serve as the prototypical danger situation, it can do so only because it is so construed after the fact—*nachträglich:*

> The situation of privation, in which stimuli reach an un-pleasurable magnitude and intensity without an ability to cope with them psychically and thus provide for their discharge, must represent to the infant a situation analogous to the birth experience, a repetition of the danger situation; what the two situations have in common is the economic disturbance brought about by an increase in stimuli demanding some disposition be made of them, this common factor hence being the very es-sence of the "danger." (ibid.)

The origin of danger lies in its repetition, in a later moment that fashions a retrospective prototype. The essence of danger is para-doxically established by analogy. The commotion of the hungry in-fant is the sign of an anxiety produced by the eruption of the past into the present in the form of its "meaning." But this infantile anxiety is still a reaction to a recognition of a danger; we have yet to follow the move toward the notion of anxiety as a defensive anticipation:

> Along with the experiencing of the fact that an external and perceptible object may put an end to the danger situation remi-niscent of birth, there takes place a displacement of the content of the danger from the economic situation to that which occa-sions it, namely object loss. The perception of the absence of the mother now becomes the danger at the appearance of which the infant gives the signal of anxiety, even before the economic situation which is feared has arisen. This change represents a first great step in advance in the economy of self-preservation. (77)

What was first perceived to be the effect of a repetition that consti-tuted its origin after the fact as a birth trauma, is now no longer the *result* of that repetition, but the *anticipation* of its possibility. The ob-ject of anxiety shifts from the economic situation of hunger to the disappearance of the mother, a shift made possible by displacement. Working by association, like the figure of metonymy, displacement moves anxiety into the anticipatory mode: it makes anxiety anxious. This "first great step in advance" for "self-preservation" has the effect of throwing the self in advance of itself, anxiously reading the world in anticipation of the repetition of the past. The "signal of anxiety," *Angstsignal,* is the signal of a displacement, the signal that displacement is installed in the subject. In a later addition to his essay, Freud stresses the function of displacement in the *angst* of anxiety:

> But the crux of the matter is the initial displacement of the anxiety reaction from its origin in the situation of helplessness to the anticipation of the latter, the danger situation. There then ensue the further displacements from the danger itself to that which occasions the danger, namely, object loss and the modifications thereof already mentioned. (115)

This last sentence adumbrates the potentially endless metonymical chain along which displacement will fix anxiety, to fashion the future as the repetition of the past in symbolic form. Anxiety is the signal that a temporal structure exists in the place of the self: a structure where meaning arrives to the self *après coup,* and authorizes an anticipatory representation of the future. Such a temporality is "crucial" to the preservation of the self—a task that the self manages by throwing the shape of the past always ahead of itself, by means of displacement. The signal of anxiety testifies to the necessary conditions for the moderately miserable, anxiously Oedipal, interminably resistant Freudian subject, whose present forever escapes him in the awaiting of an anterior future.

In the essay on laughter, Baudelaire picks up the character of Virginie and has her submit to a certain violation in the "here" of his text. Her fall into his essay causes a violent disjointing of the simplicity of her present, and the sense of scandal and anxiety that she feels is a signal, in affective terms, of the dispersal of "joy"—of self-presence—in and through the temporal structure of the *comique significatif.* If I have discussed Freud's comments on anxiety at some length, it is to suggest that both Freud and Baudelaire wrote on the relations among self, time, and sense—and that both were concerned with the lag or gap that inheres in the self's sense of itself as sense, direction, meaning, or *telos*. Since Baudelaire did not possess the conceptual terminology of a Viennese doctor of our century, he stole his language by stealing Virginie, in order to do awful things to her. And since he did not "know" what Freud was about, having never read him, Baudelaire wrote himself directly into the mode of the significantly comical, where sense arrives *nachträglich*. But does he merely "lend" himself to a Freudian reading of Virginie's loss? Up until now I have focused on his negative and easy thrusting of Bernardin's heroine into the world of modern Paris, and to that extent a certain Freudian script seems to account for her fate there. But Baudelaire continues his interlude with Virginie at the same time that he dismisses her from the essay:

> Sans doute, que Virginie reste à Paris et que la science lui vienne, le rire lui viendra; nous verrons pourquoi. (529)

Let us examine more closely this turn toward prophecy, keeping in mind the question not only of what Virginie means in the essay, but of what she does.

The Comical as Method

> "L'être-pour-la-mort" de Heidegger, loin de caractériser la possibilité authentique, ne représenterait donc pour Baudelaire qu'une imposture de plus. Nous n'avons pas devant nous la mort, mais l'existence qui, si loin que j'avance, est toujours devant et, si bas que je m'enfonce, est toujours plus bas et, si irréellement que je m'affirme (par exemple dans l'art), infeste cette irréalité d'une absence de réalité qui est encore l'existence.
> —Maurice Blanchot, *La Part du feu*

Baudelaire's prophecy invokes a third moment in the parable of Virginie, and thus prevents her story from being contained within a two-part structure of a "before" and "after," an "innocence" and "fall," or a "joy" and "anxiety." At the same time, however, his narration of her adventures in modern Paris ends with that prophecy, so that she disappears from the essay, borne off in an attitude of tension toward the future. As a result, the work of fulfilling the prophecy is no longer that of the writer-narrator, and becomes the task of the reader. That shifting of roles is implicit in the prophecy's final statement, "Nous verrons pourquoi": as the narrative about Virginie ends, "we" are called upon to fill in the final episode. Since we can no longer follow the perambulations of a character in a narrative, we are forced to reread and rethink the parable as a whole. We then, as readers, are also placed within the *nachträglich* structure of comical signification.

Virginie appears on the scene of the essay as a figure of "absolute naïveté," borrowed from the text of Bernardin de Saint-Pierre. Uprooted, and coerced to play a role in Baudelaire's essay, this figure comes to participate in an eccentric relation to meaning upon confronting the duplicitous type of representation called caricature. The caricature that she confronts is specified as lewd, and her encounter with it is thus imbued with the resonance of the discovery of castration—a fantasmatically charged scene, or scenario, in which gender is assigned to the subject through the mediation of a cultural world of signs. In the "here" of the essay, Virginie's transparent and unisexed bond with humanity is beclouded by the separation, sexuality, and cultural overdetermination that inheres in funny smut.[20] The "sudden folding of wings" that results injects an undeniable element of pathos in the story of this figure whom we recognize as having once been joyously at home in the text of Bernardin. In the "here" of the essay we witness her fall into anxiety, and then are asked to "see" how she will come to laugh.

We can begin to envisage her laughter by noting that "here" functions not only to dramatize Virginie's move into the modern and urban world, but also to stress the particular space within the essay where her story is told. As we have seen, Virginie is introduced as a first example, immediately after the essay's curious—abysmal— meditation on beginnings, sources, reflections, and citations. In this essay, where laughter and the comical come to sound like screens for writing and meaning, Virginie falls from joy into anxiety within a textual space that is opened by no little apparent anxiety about the connection between writing and full meaning. And her Fall within this anxious space results from encountering a text—caricature—whose essence is the mediation and deferral of its sense. After the Fall, she is occluded in the same gesture by which the reader is enjoined to fulfill the prediction that she will learn to laugh. The example of Virginie is withdrawn, and we are left to think through her laughter by reconsidering her story in the light of its final prophecy—by rereading the essay's "here" as a textual space.

The sole clue to Virginie's laughter occurs in the following passage, where Baudelaire recalls her briefly:

> Et voyez comme tout s'accorde: quand Virginie, déchue, aura baissé d'un degré en pureté, elle commencera à avoir l'idée de sa propre supériorité, elle sera plus savante au point de vue du monde, et elle rira. (530)

Behind this psychological portrayal of laughter lies an insight into how the assumption of a certain "purity" has determined our response to Virginie's Fall. The pathos evoked in the sudden folding of the wings of this "great figure" depends upon our recognizing her as an intertextual identity—as *the* Virginie from Bernardin's novel. It is this prior identity, this exemplary intactness, that guarantees the code of violation on which her story in the "here" of the essay is grounded. Baudelaire's claim of violence, and his example of violation, depend on our recognizing Virginie as stolen, uprooted, out of place, or *unheimlich* in Heidegger's sense of not-being-at-home.[21] Her identity as "la virginale Virginie" enables the violation to be played out "here," to the apparent satisfaction of an overriding sense of anxiety. And laughter, we are told, can only result from a further, additional loss of her assumed purity.

"La virginale Virginie": Baudelaire's hyperbolic epithet spins about itself with the same vertiginous redundancy that we encountered in "absolument châtré." If, in our reading, we take this sardonic repetition as a feint that should arouse suspicion, we might begin to suspect our assumption of Virginie's initial inviolateness. Suppose, for instance, that she were not a simple example, not an intertextual *identity,* from the very start: suppose she were a mask, behind which we find, not the sentimentality of Bernardin, but rather the implacable logic of Pascal, whom we have found more directly cited elsewhere in the essay. Is not Virginie's loss in the "here" of Baudelaire's text already prefigured in Pascal's observation:

> Que chacun examine ses pensées, il les trouvera toujours oc-cupées au passé et à l'avenir. Nous ne pensons presque point au présent; et si nous y pensons, ce n'est que pour en prendre la lumière pour disposer de l'avenir. Le présent n'est jamais notre fin.
>
> Le passé et le présent sont nos moyens; le seul avenir est notre fin. Ainsi nous ne vivons jamais, mais nous espérons de vivre; et, nous disposant toujours à être heureux, il est inévi-table que nous ne le soyons jamais.[22]

Pascal's discussion of anxiety, or "inquiétude," is centered on the es-cape of the present in anticipation of a *futur-antérieur* modeled on the past and forever in suspense. And Baudelaire's parable of the Fall of Virginie is a dramatization of Pascal's analysis of the human experi-ence of time, but it is more than merely an enlivened repetition of a psychological analysis of anxiety. By writing out the Pascalian in-tertext *through* Virginie, he complicates the sense of presence by which that emblematic name might intend a simple and single refer-ent. Virginie names a Romantic intertext, but that name functions only as a mask, behind which lies another intertext. Virginie does not arrive on the scene of the essay's "here" as a joyous self-identity, but rather as the self-conscious inscription of how that "here" describes a space shared among a plurality of writers. The Pascalian intertext disclosed in our rethinking of the parable initi-ates Virginie into the realm of the comical by revealing her textual impurity: what had appeared to indicate a simple exchange between two writers now imperfectly masks a more general prostitution—Baudelaire's term for art itself.[23]

In other words, Baudelaire's prophecy that Virginie will come to laugh by achieving a further loss of purity is fulfilled when the reader understands the degree to which his own assumption of a prior identity for Virginie has enabled the story of her Fall. Reread-ing and rethinking Baudelaire's mobilization of Virginie leads us to question how a "great figure" like Virginie can ever enjoy the happy state of self-identity: her very status as a *literary* allusion, her easy availability as a figure, cause her always to be someplace other than simply *chez elle*. We can then draw two inferences from the narration of her Fall and the prophecy of her laughter.

First, as an exemplary name whose referent is potentially human, Virginie's story describes the fall from the narcissistic plenitude of "joy" into the mediated and disjointed space of cultural signification. In this eccentric space, anxiety signals the self's defensive stance against the possibility for which the narcissistic loss can serve as the pattern—of separation, helplessness, mediation, and scattering. In this space, anxiety is anxious precisely to the extent it projects castration into the future as a horrific potentiality. Laughter, on the other hand, quells anxiety in the recognition that the anticipated danger has already, fundamentally, happened: just as Virginie has always been tainted by her figural impurity, so the human subject is constituted through the very castration that it fears as a future possibility. To laugh is to abandon the anxious anticipation of castration, and to assume a different relation to it. In this relation, castration is understood as a constitutive element of human subjectivity—as a concomitant effect of the infant's accession to language. Such a relation to castration is commonly identified as "feminine," since it entails a recognition and acceptance of a founding loss. Such an understanding of castration leads Serge Leclaire to write in "Sexuality: A Fact of Discourse" that

> For man, the possession of the penis, which is highly cathected, serves as a screen denying the fundamental character of castration. Man comes to believe that he has not been castrated. Even psychoanalysts don't recognize the phallus as absent. They think that castration is a fact for woman and that man only fears castration. (46)

No longer defined as either a future danger or a gender-specific threat, but instead as the condition of possibility for language, castration loosens the notions of "masculine" and "feminine" from their biological reference, and establishes them as attitudes toward the fact that the phallus exists only on the level of the symbolic. The "masculine" is then to be defined as the attitude of denial, resulting in the anxious anticipation of the *déjà-perdu*. To speak of a "feminine" relation to castration does not necessarily refer us to a woman's point of view, but rather to an attitude beyond, or other than, denegation and anxiety. Thus Baudelaire's essential laughter—the signal of this alternative relation to castration—must come to a feminine character, to *the* feminine name *par excellence*. Insofar as that name gestures toward human experience, toward the psychology of laughter, the parable of Virginie ends by showing how laughter can come to transcend, after the fact, the castration anxiety that had initially seemed to be the parable's final truth.

But, as we have seen elsewhere, psychology is not Baudelaire's sole concern in the essay on laughter, which leads me to my second point. Virginie enters the already anxious "here" of the essay as a name that gestures not only toward human experience, but toward the world of other texts—the world whose obsessive and pervasive power was explored in the essay's opening. And her parable is structured by both narrative and prophecy, so that the reader must arrive at its end by returning to its beginning, to disclose the Pascal that is behind the Bernardin that is behind the Baudelaire. Virginie's initiation into the realm of the comical depends upon a display of a complex intertextuality, and upon a series of demaskings that cannot be guaranteed to have a proper order nor a fixed terminus. The device, whether intentional or not, of engaging the reader to understand Virginie's impurity as her intertextual fragmentation, calls especial attention to the impurity of Baudelaire's text itself: his parable marks and re-marks its commerce among other texts, enjoining the reader to do the same. Thus, in the movement by which Virginie is initiated into the comical, the text displays its own comical structure of deferral and fragmentation. The parable becomes a textual performance of its theme, in which Virginie mimes the elements of reflexivity at the same time that she conveys a psychological proposition.

Of course the comicality of which I am speaking is not that of the merely funny, but of the *comique significatif*. Since the comical and the significant are associated categories in the essay, the elliptical parable seems to align more strongly than ever the notion of a certain laughter with a kind of writing. If laughter is the admission of the comical as disjoining, mediation, and deferral, then a laughter could inhere in the impurity—the textuality—of writing. Virginie laughs upon discovering that both her subjectivity, as a "character," and her textuality, as a "great figure," imply a loss of privacy, of an interiority to which sense can safely return. If such laughter evinces, as Baudelaire claims, a superiority, it is then a paradoxical superiority—similar to what is called elsewhere "la conscience dans le Mal."[24]

Virginie may learn to laugh in the essay on laughter, but were she to cry instead, the essay says, it would come to the same thing: both laughter and tears are redemptive, for each disrupts the static tension of anxiety:

> Et remarquez que c'est aussi avec les larmes que l'homme lave les peines de l'homme, que c'est avec le rire qu'il adoucit quelquefois son coeur et l'attire; car les phénomènes engendrés par la chute deviendront les moyens du rachat. (528)

The commensurability of laughter and tears invites us to turn to a poem about tears, in order better to gloss the overlayered parable of Virginie. In that poem it is more explicitly a question of artful masking, and of the art of demasking. There exist, as we shall see, other parallels between the poem and the texts I have been discussing: as in "Un Voyage à Cythère," the poem sets into motion a play among voices—a play indicated by dashes throughout the text and contained only by the pronoun *nous*; like the essay's choice of Virginie, the poem chooses as its referent another work of art—a statue by Ernest Christophe; and like the parable of Virginie, the poem thematizes a "complication of painful elements"—progressing from an initial assumption of unity, to a perception of duality, and then to a dispersion toward the future. Finally, it should be pointed out that the poem occurs in *Les Fleurs du Mal* near the end of a cycle of poems that all pose the question of the nature of the beautiful in the work of art. The poem is, of course, "Le Masque":

STATUE ALLÉGORIQUE DANS LE GOÛT DE LA RENAISSANCE

A Ernest Christophe, statuaire

Contemplons ce trésor de grâces florentines;
Dans l'ondulation de ce corps musculeux
L'Elégance et la Force abondent, soeurs divines.

Cette femme, morceau vraiment miraculeux,
Divinement robuste, adorablement mince,
Est faite pour trôner sur des lits somptueux,
Et charmer les loisirs d'un pontife où d'un prince.

—Aussi, vois ce souris fin et voluptueux
Où la Fatuité promène son extase;
Ce long regard sournois, langoureux et moqueur;
Ce visage mignard, tout encadré de gaze,
Dont chaque trait nous dit avec un air vainqueur:
"La Volupté m'appelle et l'amour me couronne!"
A cet être doué de tant de majesté
Vois quel charme excitant la gentillesse donne!
Approchons, et tournons autour de sa beauté.

O blasphème de l'art! ô surprise fatale!
La femme au corps divin, promettant le bonheur,
Par le haut se termine en monstre bicéphale!

—Mais non! ce n'est qu'un masque, un décor suborneur,
Ce visage éclairé d'une exquise grimace,
Et, regarde, voici, crispée atrocement
La véritable tête, et la sincère face
Renversée à l'abri de la face qui ment.
Pauvre grande beauté! le magnifique fleuve
De tes pleurs aboutit dans mon coeur soucieux;
Ton mensonge m'enivre, et mon âme s'abreuve
Aux flots que la Douleur fait jaillir de tes yeux!

—Mais pourquoi pleure-t-elle? Elle, beauté parfaite
Qui mettrait à ses pieds le genre humain vaincu,
Quel mal mystérieux ronge son flanc d'athlète?

—Elle pleure, insensé, parce qu'elle a vécu!
Et parce qu'elle vit! Mais ce qu'elle déplore
Surtout, ce qui la fait frémir jusqu'aux genoux,
C'est que demain, hélas! il faudra vivre encore!
Demain, après-demain et toujours!—comme nous![25]

As is often the case with Baudelaire's texts, it is diffficult to judge
how to situate the concept of a poetic stance or intention in relation
to the plurality of observations and exclamations that we find here.
Blanchot assumes that the "nous" of the final line operates to include each and any reader within a statement on the human condition; that assumption consequently allows "Le Masque" to play a
key role in Blanchot's defense of Baudelaire against Sartre.[26] The
polemical urgency of his argument, however, draws him to overlook
another, and perhaps a more evident, possibility: since the poem is
no more than an exchange among voices, the final phrase "comme
nous" has at least as much power to enclose and to bring into relief
the highly self-conscious facticity of the text as it does to offer those
voices as representations of you or me. The self-enclosure and self-
referentiality of "comme nous" is heightened by the poem's subtitle,
whose lack of an initial prepositional phrase like *sur une* allows the
word "statue" ambiguously to describe both the poem's referent and
the poem itself. That is, the subtitle draws attention to the statuesque
nature of verse—its hewn, poised, and artificial qualities—at the
same time that it suggests that the poem is about a statue. The poem
is both prompted by a statue and similar to a statue: a poem about
a statuesque mode of being-about. The ambiguous subtitle and
the final likening of the statue to "us"—the poem's component
voices—thus frame the text as explicitly self-referential, as a "verbal
icon" that comments upon its own iconic standing through the mediation of Christophe's three-dimensional icon.

Let us consider briefly the result of the statue's mediation in the
poetic text. Baudelaire had seen a statuette, titled *La Comédie humaine,* in Christophe's studio. That piece is described in the *Salon de
1859,* where Baudelaire regrets that Christophe had not cast and ex-
hibited the work.[27] The statuette showed a vigorous and robust nude
who, when viewed from the front, presented "un visage souriant et
mignard, un visage de théâtre." A shift in the spectator's position
revealed that smiling face to be a mask, behind which lay "le secret
de l'allégorie, la morale de la fable, je veux dire la véritable tête
révulsée, se pâmant dans les larmes et l'agonie." The statuette, in
other words, dramatized the classic opposition between appearance
and truth, the artificial and the real, Art and Nature: that set of oppositions constituted *La Comédie humaine.* Baudelaire, however, does

not revive these oppositions, for he does not write a poem about a woman whose truth tries to hide behind a "visage de théâtre"; instead he writes (about) a statue, and more precisely, about the sequential perception of the statue. The set of oppositions is thus displaced into the sole realm of art, so that the categories of Truth and Appearance are shifted toward categories that we might call True Appearance and Apparent Appearance, or Appearance-in-Time and Immediate Appearance. Concomitantly, Christophe's title, redolent of the problem of the Real, is replaced by "Le Masque," imbuing the text with the atmosphere of the theater—which is to say, with the problem of appearance. How does a work of art—a statue that is like a poem, or a poem that is like a statue—appear? How does it perdure? What is the time of its appearance, and its appearance through time? How might a text both smile and cry? It is the mediation of Christophe's statue that allows such questions to govern the poem, and that aligns this text, as a meditation on writing, with the essay on laughter.

The statue, then, comes to stand for the verse that evokes it, and the poem comes to dramatize its own mode of being through the sequence of commentaries on the statue. There are three moments in that dramatization. At first, the work exudes an "Elegance" and "Force" that inhere in its formal integrity: the rhythmic and sonorous qualities of verse, "l'ondulation de ce corps musculeux," effect what Nietzsche calls a compelling of the gods, or a binding of the future.[28] The face of the work smiles with the beatitude of joy, as appearance and being seem to form a seamless whole. Then, in a second moment, the formal illusion is broken. The formality of the work may mask but cannot annul all that is dross, sedimented, and other in the language that the poem erects as the simulacrum of full speech. Behind the forceful mask, the text exudes its tears.

I will come back to the relation between these two faces, but let us note beforehand that the third moment of the dramatization shifts the terms of the discussion. At the end of the poem, it is no longer a question of a spatial metaphor—of a spectator's turning about the work in an arc that mirrors the perversity of language. Now the inability of the work to maintain a simple smile is grounded in the fact of its existence in time, which is made explicit by the explanatory repetition of *vivre* in three tenses. That repetition moves from past to present to future, implying that it is not merely the determinations and overdeterminations of an historical past that impede the self-coincidence of the work in a present moment, but that it is especially the way in which any such moment of apperception faces the work as an uncertain future. The work is not bound toward the finality of death, but rather toward an infinite set of interpretations that will always disclose more and less than the full containment of sense to which the work aspires. The poem's final exclamation, "comme nous," asserts the identification of statue and text; the text is not only statuesque by virtue of its formal, printed materiality, but it is like this particular statue—split between an elegant surface and a tearful subsurface—through the loss of contact with the authorial voice, the loss that allows the text to stand as "itself." The shift from spatial to temporal terms completes the dramatization of the "existence," in Blanchot's sense, of the written text, outside the "irreal" fullness of a poetic ideal.

The emblematic power of the statue to figure the existence of writing is greatest precisely in the space where the statue is not: in the gap between the two faces. Baudelaire's text will turn the statue's blank space of disjunction into a relation, as we shall see. In lines 20 through 28, a voice avidly claims a clear difference in kind between the two faces. The one

> . . . n'est qu'un masque, un décor suborneur,
> Ce visage éclairé d'une exquise grimace. . . .

Behind this mask of art lies

> La véritable tête, et la sincère face
> Renversée à l'abri de la face qui ment.

This complete valorization of the statue's underface leads to an exclamation of sadistic ecstasy, whose language curiously anticipates that of *L'Héautontimorouménos:*

> et mon âme s'abreuve
> Aux flots que la Douleur fait jaillir de tes yeux!

This swoon over the tearful Truth is cut short by another voice, but more important, the excited language in which the disjunction between the two faces is claimed ends up by complicating that disjunction. On the one hand, the "véritable face" is found in the *shelter* of the mask, as if its tears could only appear, and appear as truth, by virtue of the mask that imperfectly conceals them. Without the mask, the crying face might itself appear, as it often does in Baudelaire, to be no more than a mask. The mask thus guarantees, in its slippage, the attribution of truth to the surface beneath it. On the other hand, the mask is called "un décor suborneur"—a phrase whose etymology calls into question the superfluity and inessentiality of its object. That is, *suborneur* derives from the Latin *suborno,* meaning both "to equip, to fit out," and "to incite secretly." This divagation of sense in turn is caused by a basic ambiguity in the root verb *orno,* which means both "to furnish with necessary equipment" and "to adorn with mere decoration." That ambiguity persists in the archaic sense of "ornament" as "useful equipment." Within the phrase "un décor suborneur" we find inscribed an ambiguity that ranges as far back as the Greek verb *kosmein,* meaning both "to establish an order, a cosmos, that overcomes chaos" and "to add cosmetic adornment." The "décor suborneur" thus resonates as both a seductive trapping, a secondary and illusive decoration, and a primary addition required in order to be at all. In the blank gap between the statue's two faces, Baudelaire's language displaces the claim of disjunction and establishes a relation of supplementarity instead.

As a meditation on the mode of being of its own language, "Le Masque" suggests that poetry might reside in the space between its fetishistic mask and the face of a "mal mystérieux" that eats away at language. In this plurivocal text, the notion of poetry as expressive utterance has little place. Neither do description and evocation, for if Christophe's statue serves as an initial referent, the referential function of the text cedes to a self-reflexivity that turns the description of the statue toward an intimation of the uncertain future into which the text is cast. Self-reflexivity does not lead, though, to certain self-knowledge, but only to this admission—avowal and entry—of uncertainty within language. It is as if Christophe's statue figured for the poet the failure of poetry as a totalization of sense. The poetic text does not know itself, coincide with itself, or offer itself as the mastery of meaning. It can offer only a smiling mask, imperfectly concealing the tears that betoken the presence of the other within the one. But if poetry cannot be erected to the status of a fetish, neither is it derided as illusion or error, for it is the smile of the mask that guarantees the value of those tears. Poetry becomes a formal desire, or a formalization of desire, whose object lies elsewhere than in fulfillment. And in the same way that the object of desire cannot be localized in the Real without the mediation of the signs that make up fantasy, poetry cannot explore the raw uncertainty of language as such, without the mask of an ideal of full containment. "Le Masque" does not offer a choice between the mask of art and the face of the real; it displays instead the necessary relation between the two.

"Le Masque" works out the poetic implications of the problem of anxiety as it is posed in the essay on laughter. Virginie's laughter, we have seen, signals the admission of a specific impurity in both the existence of the subject and of the text. The veiled tears of "Le Masque" function similarly. The poem thus indicates a poetic stance that locates itself outside the circuit of sincerity and irony, to assume a comic relation to the signification of the text. Poetry here is engaged in neither the manic denial of the fetishist, nor the negative celebration of the ironist, for both of those positions are ridden with an anxiety over the control of meaning. To position the poet outside that anxious circuit, to allow laughter and tears to inhere within the poetic project, amounts, perhaps, to granting a certain initiative to the uncertainty of words.

Impure Poetry

> L'éphémère ébloui vole vers toi, chandelle,
> Crépite, flambe et dit: Bénissons ce flambeau!
> —*Hymne à la Beauté*

At the beginning of this chapter, I suggested that Baudelaire's fascination with the English Pierrot had something to do with how that version of the Guignol character might figure for the poet an attitude toward poetry, or a relation between the poet and his writing. I also suggested that the absoluteness of Pierrot's comicality echoed the hyperbolic absoluteness of the Cytherean's castration in the revised version of the "Voyage à Cythère." My reading of the essay on laughter then led me to infer that a notion of "pure poetry" forms the backdrop against which Baudelaire wrote his "physiologie du rire," as he sometimes called it. The essay performs as if he were writing out a certain anxiety concerning writing by borrowing the language of the contemporary genre of the *physiologie* in order to confront that anxiety and, perhaps, to deflate it. Using that language to write about laughter, the poet obliquely acknowledges the gap that yawns between the subject's desire for language to reflect no more than a full containment of sense, and language's need to thwart that desire in order to be understood at all—since its interpretability is conventionally determined, temporally complex, and historically sedimented. Pure poetry—where laughter lacks—is a concept that reflects the nostalgic longing for a narcissistically replete language, but is undermined in the course of the essay and shown to be a methodological impossibility. Pierrot's theft of his own severed head, Virginie's laughter, and absolute castration all figure the necessity of a poetry of impurity—a poetry that both excites the desire for purity, or full containment of sense, and that manifests the fantasmatic condition of such a desire.

The beauty of such poetry resides neither in the limpidity of its expressivity, nor in the formalism of the language that embodies it, for both pure expression and mere form are versions of a reduction to simple sense. The one is no more than the erection of a sense among the tensions at work in the verbal icon, while the other, like Flaubert's famous book about nothing, is the negation of the former: the erection of an icon devoid of meaning save for its very erection. In the essay on laughter, beauty is linked to the work's resistance to recuperation, where recuperation is understood as the determination of reference, be it external reference or self-reference. Caricature is beautiful when its external referentiality is not obliterated, but short-circuited, by a hilarity that prevents its being completely consumed by its referent. Similarly, the impure poem is beautiful because it is a formal tendency toward a meaning other than itself, yet is no more a simply meaningful formulation than it is a meaningless form. Laughter, in this sense, celebrates the will to contain meaning in language, but celebrates that effort *as* will, or as desire.

If we return our attention now to the space between the two versions of the "Voyage à Cythère," we will see there the space of the interference of laughter. Consider, first, the representation of truth in this voyage, a representation that is certified as truthful in the assertion that "mon image" is discovered in the hanged man. The power that this specular captation can assert over the reader surfaces in an observation like: "the poet has recognized his own destiny in the fate of the hanged man."[29] We have already seen the extent to which the revised "Voyage" problematizes the function of a "speaker" in the poem, and by extension the possibility of identifying "the poet" as a localized voice within this fragmented discourse. The polyphony of the text functions to resist any unifying reading of the poem, by bringing into relief the degree to which that unification of sense is a reflection of the reader's desire as much as it is a necessary or constitutive element of the poem. But the text invites such a unification *while* it disrupts its possibility. The specular path to sense is deployed as a trap, and when a reader identifies "the poet" or some other heuristic construct as the singular object of a meaningful mirroring, he does so by asking the text to mirror the "truth" that he brings to it. The reader then risks being caught in the specular fixity that the text both asserts and undercuts. The text proffers an identity that is given in a mirror—"mon image"—and also the possibility of a textual identity that can become a reader's mirror; yet it cannot be said to propose mirroring as a truthful operation, since any whole and proper image that it is made to reflect will necessitate the repression of its impure laughter, its comicality and noncoincidence.

But if the text resists being read as a monument to self-recognition, might it not yet be allegorized as a reflection upon the conditions of its own writing? Might not Baudelaire have in mind the mutilation of a poetic father figure—a Hugo *sacerdote*—when he revises his early poem for publication? These questions presuppose the pertinency of a model whereby the rewriting of the poem would entail primarily the shadowy working out of a certain anxiety of influence, so that "papa" might be read beneath the figure of the hanged man. Such a reading would itself reside in anxiety; by insisting on the primacy of an Oedipal theory of poetry, it would reduce the hyperbolic insistence of "absolument châtré" to the mere index of a family romance. It would have to ignore the revision's carefully prepared progress toward the deflationary power of that phrase, remaining blind to the poem's focal concentration upon a phrase of excessive meaning, in order to distill its anxious masculine sense from the text's display of disruptive and feminine comicality.

Either class of reading would not so much fix the mirroring relation in the text as it would end up by reflecting the desire of the reader to put a stop to its circulation of possible senses. And it would do so by refusing to see that the mutilation of the hapless *pendu* is not simply contained by the text, but suffered by it as well, in the dispersion of its voice. Were a fantasmatic Hugo the object of such hyperbolic violence—the victim of a kind of poetic overkill— it would be difficult to claim that Baudelaire thus assumes a dominance in relation to him, since the fate of the victim is shared by the text itself. The *clinamen,* or corrective trope, that informs the text aims at Hugo no more than the earlier version set out to correct Nerval.[30]

The object of the clinamen seems indeed to be the trope of allegory itself or the trope's tendency to fix the flow of the world in a relation of correspondence. Starting with the earlier version of the poem, which I have described as an hysterical identification, the process of revising the text turns a specular duality into something more akin to a hall of mirrors. If Hugo becomes inscribed as a palimpsest beneath the *ridicule pendu*—and we have sufficient evidence for a feasible argument to that effect—then his virtual presence in the text further disrupts the possibility of deciding on the point where the reflections of correspondences ought to stop. A schematic representation of only the basic mirroring relations in the revised text would have to show an endless cycle:

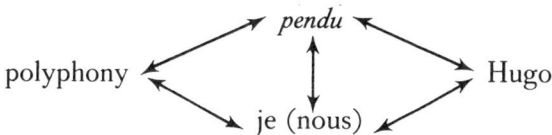

This schema does not try to account graphically for the sundry secondary correspondences in the text. A complete mirror of mirroring would have to include various birds, the *plus grande bête,* the sea and the sky, for example. But the schema does suggest the way in which the revised text turns a specular duality into a kind of reflecting machine. The circular structure of reflections suggests that any given statement concerning the sense of the text—"The hanged man becomes the image of the speaker's fate"; "Castration is reflected in the fragmentation of the speaker's voice"; "The inhabitant of Cythera becomes associated with the hated yet revered inhabitant of Jersey"—creates only a momentary stoppage of a continual flow. Meaning, in other words, surfaces as an *effect* from the text; it is not the force that drives the text toward closure.

The circulation of correspondence in a cycle of sense seems especially strange, or perhaps we should rather say resistant and beautiful, in a text that calls itself a "voyage," and that builds itself around a primary metaphor of self-constitution—the discovery of castration. The poem proposes the most self-satisfying of journeys only to displace continually the points that enable its trajectory. As Baudelaire writes in his note to Gautier, "it would be nice to find" a single point of departure for the "Voyage," and a unique destination as well. But a simple path toward the final sense of the text cannot be traced without stifling a certain laughter that derives from its comical structure of signification, sending the reader to another place, just when he anxiously hopes that he has arrived at a solid destination.

3

Without-Within

A Tentative Poetics

> Ouverture tentée dans l'épaisseur du
> monde.
> —Yves Bonnefoy, *Théâtre*

Toward the end of an article that shows how "Obsession" reads and undermines the sonnet "Correspondances," Paul de Man observes:

> Whenever we encounter a text such as "Obsession"—that is, whenever we read—there is always an infratext, a hypogram like "Correspondances" underneath. Stating this relationship, as we just did, in phenomenal, spatial terms, or in phenomenal, temporal terms—"Obsession," a text of recollection and elegiac mourning *adds* remembrance to the flat surface of time in "Correspondances"—produces at once a hermeneutic, fallacious lyrical reading of the unintelligible.[1]

The infratext undoes, and is undone by, the resolution which the text at hand purports to assert; to phenomenolize the relation between them is to tame and thematize it under the sign of noncontradiction. De Man and others have taught us that reading consists largely in attention to the ineradicability of the unintelligible—to the ghostly whispers always already at work within the text that one reads. Whenever we read "Un Voyage à Cythère" we uncover its palimpsestic double, the hypogram that refers us once again to Nerval and to Hugo, and which finally poses the problem of just where or how one might speak of a single poem beneath that title. The shadow of unintelligibility that is cast over "Un Voyage à Cythère" adumbrates some profound uncertainty about the stability of meaning, and self-meaning, in the face of time, death, and contingency. The poem becomes possessed, in other words, with a degree of self-reflexivity that calls into question the very notion of self—be it the psychological identity of a speaker or the ontological perdurance of a poem. Where De Man, as cited above, is concerned with the subtle relation between two poetic identities, I am arguing that other poems might directly challenge the notion of poetic identity itself, preferring an uncertain and plural status to some pretension toward identity and contained meaning. The "Voyage" playfully asks us to state the space, sense, or time of its text and in so doing launches us on the very voyage toward sense and identity that it both presupposes and calls into question.

De Man's extraordinary reading of "Correspondances" is at odds with prior interpretations of the sonnet as an aesthetic program. His argument hinges on the dual function of the adverb *comme*, which can either assert positive homogeneity with the force of simile or merely introduce instances of potentially endless enumeration. At its strongest the adverb can assert identical qualities between a pair of referents, stabilizing them in their reciprocal likeness, and at its weakest it can only offer one or more examples to confirm a general proposition. He shows how the repeated use of the word in "Correspondances" deteriorates from the first, strong sense to the second one, subverting rhetorically the very notion of "correspondence" that the poem has been thought to proclaim as the basis of a poetics. Congruent substitutions devolve into a series of examples as the sonnet closes, and de Man remarks:

> That the very word on which these substitutions depend would just then lose its syntactical and semantic univocity is too striking a coincidence not to be, like pure chance, beyond the control of the author and reader. (250)

My reading of the essay on laughter would lead me to ascribe such moments in Baudelaire's verse to something other than what de Man calls, elsewhere in his essay, "a purely linguistic disruption" (260). I want to assert a poetic space between the conscious delusion of mastery, on the one hand, and the effective force of mere chance, on the other. Through "Un Voyage à Cythère" and its related texts, I have made a case for the existence of a mode of poetry in Baudelaire that ends up subverting the iconic stance of the poem by denying the stasis of sense. Through the essay on laughter, I have sought to show how the poet's discussion of comicality screens an almost anxious exploration of the escape of language from the control of an ego aspiring to some "pure" expression of the subjective experience of sense. Baudelaire's discussion of laughter broadens toward a meditation on other eruptive and disruptive experiences that belie subjective and conscious control: it quickly becomes a meditation on fallenness, formulating itself around the thematics of castration, its vicissitudes, and avatars. But if the essay goes on to consider obliquely the otherness of language, the deferral of sense, the noncoincidence that makes up the texture of the self, and the intertextual determination of the possibilities of expression, it desires nonetheless to understand laughter as the means of a certain redemption or as a sublimation of anxiety. Thus Pierrot appears at the end of the essay as a graphic and overdetermined figure of the writerly stance. Thus also Virginie assumes the comicality of which she is momentarily the victim through a descent beyond mere impurity, toward the cleansing realm of laughter.

Laughter is, then, the topic through which contingency is inscribed in a poetics. It is an obsessive notion for the poet because it is a phenomenon that ultimately impinges on writing, and Baudelaire's essay unpacks the relation between his obsessive topic and his (pre)occupation. Then, read in the light of the essay on laughter, "Le Masque" becomes a poetic declaration that poetry might begin to explore, rather than repress, the gap between its smiling pose of language restored to an original integrity and its inevitable excessive escape—in the form of tears or laughter—from the control of a subject for whom language is not an expressive, secondary medium, but rather the very condition of its possibility. One mode, then, of Baudelaire's poetry might be said to focus on the uncertainty of recuperating sense to and for the self—which is to say that interpretation becomes not its aim, but its inaugural question. A poem in this mode offers itself primarily as neither an ingestion nor expression of sense and subjectivity, but rather as an aesthetic act that foregrounds the question of how language might falter in the binding of the subject to the world. The mood of such poems shifts toward the interrogative, asking the degree to which interpretation springs from desire and blindness, rather than from cognition and clarity.

We have seen how "Un Voyage à Cythère" can easily become a playful hall of mirrors rather than a gruesome display of specular fixation. Having read it as an exercise in self-correction, we find it a tricky text, whose decomposition is initiated through details—a few dashes and a hyperbolic representation of castration. The notes for the unfinished prefaces to *Les Fleurs du Mal* show the extent to which Baudelaire could conceive of poetry as a principled science, capable, he claims at one point, of being taught to anyone in twenty lessons. The hurt and bitterness behind that note are not the focus of this essay; the notion of poetry as the perpetration of certain effects of reading aligns itself interestingly, however, with another note, written in preparation for a letter to Jules Janin. Janin had extolled a happy—smiling, if you will—poetry as a desirable norm, causing Baudelaire to jot the following series of exclamations:

> Delphine Gay!—Leconte de Lisle. Le trouvez-vous bien rigolo, bien à vos souhaits, la main sur la conscience?—Et Gauthier [*sic*]? Et Valmore: et moi?—Mon truc. (*O.C.*, II, 235)

My trick. In "Un Voyage à Cythère" the *truc* is accomplished through a hyperbolic revision; in "Le Masque" it is a matter of conflating words whose resonance and etymology overdetermine sense, so that the "stasis" of meaning toward which the poem might tend is disrupted. In "Correspondances," as De Man has shown, it is the shift in the function of *comme*, moving the text from assertions of resemblance to mere enumerations of example. The poem ends just when its *transports* risk carrying the reader endlessly on: its closure is not so much a function of truth as it is an effect derived from the necessity of the sonnet form. In calling into question the possibility of its own enterprise, in failing to quell the desire aroused by its very title, asserting, rather, the role of desire in the making of sense, "Correspondances" enters what I am calling the comical mode.

To put the matter differently, we might consider a remark from Flaubert. In the first version of *L'Education sentimentale* he writes: "Et puis la poésie n'est-elle pas partout—si elle est quelque part." His remark could be read as an ironic interrogation of the *locus* of the poetic, a reading that would understand the problem of the poetic to be like that of the miraculous: if poetry, like miracles, is said to reside everywhere, then its immanent ubiquity problematizes its claim to a privileged status. If everything can be poetic, then nothing is particularly poetic in itself. The poetic becomes a pure function of the subjective power of the writer of poems—of his will to poeticize. This subjectivist reading of Flaubert brings his remark into harmony with those of the alchemical persona in Baudelaire's writing—that persona who claims to have transformed the "mud" of Paris into "gold." Flaubert, according to this reading, seems to mean: "if poetry exists at all, then it exists in everything, and it is the poet's task to bring into relief this ubiquitous quality." Poetry becomes an open field for limitless expansion or conquest. And it is not surprising to find the language of alchemy melded with the language of imperialism in Baudelaire's celebrated remark in the unfinished prefaces:

> Des poètes illustres s'étaient partagé depuis longtemps les provinces les plus fleuries du domaine poétique. Il m'a paru plaisant, et d'autant plus agréable que la tâche était plus difficile, d'extraire la *beauté* du *Mal.* (*O.C.,* I, 181)

As long as we limit the problem to the relation between the will of the poet and the site of his poetry, we are bound within the metaphorics of the imperialism cited above: the poet is the colonizer of *le nouveau,* and poetry obtains a certain commodity value on the basis of its novelty.

But Flaubert's remark might be read another way by shifting the interrogative force of the determining clause. The subjectivist reading localizes the question by stressing "anywhere" in "si elle est quelque part." Another reading could focus the question on the very being of poetry, stressing the interrogation of the verb *être* in the clause. According to this "ontological" reading, Flaubert would be asking something more akin to: "if poetry can indeed be said to *be,* must it not be capable of this state of being no matter what its subject?" This question moves away from the power of the poet to poeticize the everyday, and addresses instead the capacity of the poet to erect poetry as the reflection of being through the medium of a privileged language. It is not only the power of the poet to infer meaning and beauty from the experience of the world that is questioned, but his fundamental control over language. This reading locates the problem in relation to the language of meaning and the meaning of language, rather than in the site or subject of sense. According to this second reading, the dream of a poetic colonization takes as its object not the world of experience, but rather the experience of living through language, and leads toward the Flaubertian dream of the book about nothing or perhaps to the "sens plus pur aux mots de la tribu" of a Mallarmé.[2]

I would suppose that Baudelaire might have read Flaubert's remark both ways: that he would have had a most lively response to the notion that poetry is a matter of self-assertion through conquest, and that he would simultaneously have suspected the terms and tools of such an assertion. We find, for example, a passage from *Mon Coeur mis à nu* in which it seems to be a matter of irrealizing language and of eliminating the referential function:

> Concevoir un canevas pour une bouffonnerie lyrique ou féerique, pour une pantomime, et traduire cela en un roman sérieux. Noyer le tout dans une atmosphère anormale et songeuse,—dans l'atmosphère des *grands jours.*—Que ce soit quelque chose de berçant,—et même de serein dans la passion.—Régions de la Poésie pure. (*O.C.,* I, 664)

But to dream of a pure and irrealized construction in which poetic language would become a monument only to itself is a different matter from making such a concept the goal of a poetic project. Although the poet might conceive a strategy to shelter his language from the unforeseeable impingements of contingency, he does not necessarily deploy it: the "livre sérieux" is never written, and "pure" poetry is relegated, in the essay on laughter, to hubristic ambition.

Instead, Baudelaire maintains the desire for an imaginary control over his language—for a "supernatural" language—coextensively with a profound sense of the impossibility of centering himself sufficiently in language to exert such control, whence the necessity of what he calls the "ironic" quality of poetry. These two attitudes toward poetic language are to be maintained reciprocally, an entry in *Mon Coeur mis à nu* tells us: "Deux qualités littéraires fondamentales: surnaturalisme et ironie" (*O.C.,* I, 658). The journal entry itself does not give us much guidance in seeing how the qualities named might be juxtaposed, and seems instead to put a rhetorical device into play against a mimetic project. The passage becomes far more suggestive if we read both qualities of literature as relations toward language—relations of the poet to his language, which he might continually play off against each other.

It is the playing off that matters here. To the extent that these contradictory relations to language exist merely side by side, with the one or the other alternately predominating, the poet would find himself in the position of the fetishist. This character type interested Freud because it betrays the ego's capacity to be "split" into antithetical positions in relation to castration: the fetishist both acknowledges his perception of sexual difference and denies the female "lack" by the substitution of an ersatz object for the missing penis. He says both "yes" and "no" to the mother's body:

> It is not true that the child emerges from his experience of seeing the female parts with an unchanged belief in the woman having a phallus. He retains this belief but he also gives it up; during the conflict between the deadweight of the unwelcome perception and the force of the opposite wish, a compromise is constructed such as is only possible in the realm of unconscious modes of thought—by the primary process.[3]

The infantile experience that Freud describes here can become, he claims, the model for a more generalized process. In accordance with that model, the poet might be susceptible to alternating assertions of mastery and subjection, at times brandishing the poetic text as the ersatz object, at others denying the power of that very object. We have already seen how readings of the Baudelairean corpus can mobilize themselves around such a supposed *Spaltung*. I am concerned with that mode of his writing where the static split between wish and experience is not maintained, and where the two relations to language rather interfere. The zone of such an interference is what I am calling, following Baudelaire, the mode of the comical.

The interference between those relations to language need not be marked by any particular rhetorical device, trope, or semantic impasse. The texts that I have discussed so far do not reveal either necessary or sufficient conditions for the comical. Any text that offers itself as an interpretive gesture toward the world, but that subverts the finality of the offering, displays that refusal of self-totalization that I call comicality. The text simultaneously makes sense and indicates the facticity of its sense-making project. Neither a "sincere" nor an "ironic" text, the poem means neither to coincide with, nor countervail, its purported meaning, because its strategy lies elsewhere, in the irreification of meaning itself. The hyperbolic formulation of "absolument châtré," for example, is an index of that strategy without being a defining example of it. The poems I will consider in this chapter address the project of writing as a totalization of sense more directly than does "Un Voyage à Cythère," perhaps; but they share with that text a significant determination, a comical desire, that limits the authority of language and offers it, not as the expressive source of meaning, but as the prior condition for any sense at all. In these poems the authorial power is not abdicated—the text does not become an "open" one in Eco's "postmodernist" sense—but instead, and outside the poles of sincerity and irony, it is displayed as a construction deriving from an awkward "duel."

Surface Tension

> Plus vides, plus profonds que vous-mêmes,
> ô cieux!
> – *L'Amour du mensonge*

The poetic duel, called a "fantasque escrime," is explicitly thematized in "Le Soleil," and we will turn to it at the close of this essay to consider a rare Baudelairean portrait of the poet at work. The process of a thrust and parry with poetic sense is implicit in other texts in various ways, however, and we will take note of some of them first. Let us begin with a masterwork that undertakes to tell the story of its own creation, "Le Cygne." Margaret Gilman has called this text "the poem in which it seems to me that Baudelaire suggests most clearly the workings of the imagination."[4] If we follow her lead in approaching the poem and provisionally adopt the language of the psychology of faculties that prevailed in Baudelaire's time, we shall see that its depiction of the workings of "la reine des facultés" is far from being a rosy one. We will find that the poet who writes from the comical position of an absolute castration has created a verse text that belies his expository claims that imaginative language reflects mind as a self-governed, self-determining organ of interpretation. What the *Salon de 1859* calls the queen of the faculties is dramatized in "Le Cygne"—a poem where queens are unhappy— as a part of a less monarchical structure.

The poem opens in a complex gesture that recalls the beginning of the essay on laughter more than it does the work of a member of a visionary company. As in the essay, the poem gets underway by means of a self-assertion that is enabled only by a prior textual fragment—Vergil's tale of the Trojan heroine:

> Andromaque, je pense à vous! Ce petit fleuve,
> Pauvre et triste miroir où jadis resplendit
> L'immense majesté de vos douleurs de veuve,
> Ce Simoïs menteur qui par vos pleurs grandit,
>
> A fécondé soudain ma mémoire fertile,
> Comme je traversais le nouveau Carrousel.
> Le vieux Paris n'est plus (la forme d'une ville
> Change plus vite, hélas! que le coeur d'un mortel);

This opening begins a movement that will continue through the first of the poem's two parts, a movement which might be characterized by the sense of the Greek verb *legein,* meaning to pick out, to gather together, to give signification to, and to call by name. The apostrophe to Andromache opens a poetic space in which the speaker will gather together by means of a swan-sign the past and the present, the lived and the read, the noble and the trivial, in order to assert the perdurance of the speaking subject in the form of legible fact. The *je* that is so vigorously established by the apostrophe of the poem's first line moves at once to telling how its apostrophaic gesture has come to pass: thinking of Andromache's exile and crossing a site undergoing bourgeois *planification,* the speaker remembers a past sight on that very spot, a sight that then takes on emblematic proportion. The richness, resonance, and power of that emblem— the lost swan—serve, in turn, to affirm the constant and meaningful subjectivity of the *je* who addresses Andromache in the first place.

So quick and recuperative a paraphrase can only be offered,

though, at the expense of ignoring the care with which the poem presents its imaginative source as an indeterminate or overdetermined psychic process. The act of reading, which the poem both claims as its foundation and offers itself as to the reader of poetry, is far more heterogeneous than my simple gloss. "Le Cygne," that is, not only opens with an address to a textual trace, but it moves at once to a narration that sketches an explanation for this initial tropaic bravura.

This tropological self-consciousness first casts the speaker, not as the source of an emission, but rather as a point of intersection where Vergil's text, prior scenes, and present sights cross through the speaker, whose exact role in being thus filled with sense seems deliberately obscured by the poem's sixth line:

> Comme je traversais le nouveau Carrousel.

Does "comme je traversais" imply sequential causality, we are left to ask, or does it rather imply accidental simultaneity? The ambiguity of the conjunction in turn renders the grammatical aspect of the verb phrase "je pense à vous" somewhat unclear. Is it inchoative, meaning "I am now thinking of you because I was just crossing the Carrousel?" Or is it durative, meaning "I'm thinking of you as I was when I was crossing the Carrousel?" The ambiguous conjunction makes the answer to these questions undecidable. We cannot say whether the memory of the constructions, so like ruins, caused the speaker to ruminate on Troy and its queen, or whether such ruminations, occasioned perhaps by reading Vergil, caused the remembered construction site to take on the aspect of Trojan ruins, out of which the memory of the swan emerges. The poem's narration of its origin is illegible from the start, despite its thematic of the legibility of the speaker's world. It is difficult to say, as does F. W. Leakey for example, that Baudelaire has "made a poem simply by setting down the thoughts that freely came into his mind at the actual moment of composition."[5] The narrative that follows the opening apostrophe as if to justify it, in fact makes it impossible to declare an "actual moment" at which the poem comes into being. We are once more in the paradoxical temporality of impure poetry.

"Le Cygne," so thematically concerned with loss, lack, and the impossible return to an origin, begins, then, with a rhetorical gesture that cuts off its own discourse from a distinct causal source. "Je pense à vous" establishes a speaker who is a space of crossing as much as a crosser of spaces. The figures that traverse him in an advent of poetic sense do so in an overdetermined and unknowable manner, forming an intersection of the determined and contingent, the rational and associative, the metaphorical and metonymical. From this point of intersection, the *je* can open the poem through an apostrophe, but it cannot precisely explain that empowering tropaic gesture. We are not shown so much how one comes to write a poem as we are shown how one is overcome in the poetic process.

Undeniably, meaning does have its advent in "Le Cygne," however. The thought of Andromache in exile recalls in the speaker's memory another exile, a swan seen before, when the public square was under construction. Through the mediation of the textual trace of the queen, the swan is elevated to the status of a "mythe étrange et fatal," a sign of exile and alienation in modern, urban Paris. The one myth gives rise to another, the ancient figure allows the contemporary world to take on sense, and—not insignificantly—the speaker can experience the self as a perduring continuity in the midst of change. By means of the somewhat grotesque identification of the swan and the Trojan queen, the animal is endowed even with the gift of speech:

> Eau, quand donc pleuvras-tu? Quand tonneras-tu, foudre?

Like the poet, the swan speaks in apostrophes. For that very reason one can be tempted to read the swan, futilely and convulsively writhing, not only as the figure of physical or psychological alienation, but as that of the writing of "Le Cygne" as well. In addressing itself to water, the swan pronounces simultaneously the generalized "O" implicit in all apostrophe, as Jonathan Culler has remarked:

> Baudelaire's "Le Cygne" . . . tells of a swan who, nostalgically seeking his "beau lac natal" in a "ruisseau sans eau," supplies an "O" apostrophizing nature. . . . The coincidence of "O" and *Eau* can be variously interpreted: the nostalgic quest for a

moment or place of origin, the "eau" of a "beau lac natal," yields only an "O" of a trope; or the pun identifies the potential addressee of every apostrophe as the apostrophic "O" itself and makes every apostrophe an invocation of invocation. However one develops the implications of the pun, the result is a foregrounding of apostrophe as trope.[6]

But any identification of the swan's gesture with poetic activity will have to be, like other identifications in the poem, tenuous at best. The very word that allows the pun of "eau" and "O" names the element that works throughout the text to establish both links and differences. It is the replica of the Simoïs that provides the initial motivation for linking Andromache and the swan, since both are removed from a watery memory, and the memory of the speaker is enlivened, it is claimed, by the water of that "Simoïs menteur." The water that pours into a "mémoire fertile" to link the exiled queen and the swan then becomes a ubiquitous element in the poem. Each human exile with whom the speaker expresses solidarity is associated with the element: from Andromache swelling the little river with her tears, to the negress tramping through mud, to the wilting orphans, to the shipwrecked sailors. On the other hand, however, the swan's predicament is characterized precisely by its aridity, finely evoked in the phrase "ruisseau sans eau" and tinged with pathos in the image of bathing in powder. The element that provides the initial link between Andromache and the swan, granting the animal its mythical power, at the same time works to maintain a perhaps crucial distinction between the figure of the swan and the other exiles in the poem.

While the swan's discourse seems strikingly poetic, care must nevertheless be taken lest the distance between the swan's arid sterility and the speaker's damp fertility be too quickly effaced. Described as "ridicule et sublime," the swan is an equivocal figure whose poetic activity, such as it is, addresses natural elements. Such a stance is certainly not typical of Baudelaire, who is more likely to address Rubens or, here, Andromache or even his cat than he is to implore nature or, for that matter, to reproach the heavens. Perhaps the swan, denying the mediation of culture, is attempting some sort of pure poetry? Whether it is or not, a strong ambivalence surrounds this figure that apostrophizes nature within a text that itself addresses only another text, limiting its discourse to the watery world of human subjectivity. The fact that the poem bears a dedication to Hugo—another profoundly ambivalent figure for Baudelaire—could lead to further speculation on the equivocal value of this figure, but it is more pertinent here to consider how the swan works to comment on the act of figuration itself.

From its role as principle of memory, to that of the swan's singular lack, to that of the human associative constant, water pervades "Le Cygne." Its ubiquity suggests a submerged image underlying and generating the poem: that of the self as the repository of meaning, as the solid container into which sense flows. In part I of "Le Cygne," a satisfying plenitude is achieved in the elevation of the *cygne* to the status of a mythic *signe* comparable to, and enabled through, Andromache. But to follow the logic of this image of plenitude, any open container into which a liquid flows is never really full until it is slightly overfull, at that precarious moment when the surface tension of the liquid allows a meniscus to form. In the space between part I and part II of the poem, the meniscus gives way:

> Paris change! mais rien dans ma mélancholie
> N'a bougé! palais neufs, échafaudages, blocs,
> Vieux faubourgs, tout pour moi devient allégorie,
> Et mes chers souvenirs sont plus lourds que des rocs.

The work of allegorization that has elevated the swan to the level of a *correspondance* cannot, itself, be contained. The sense that it has allowed now overflows, and "everything" becomes invested with symbolic value. Having valorized an apparently trivial memory by lending it mythic value, the self is experienced as replete with signification. But the poem implies that such fullness is always already an overfullness and that sense tends to overflow in a process of displacement, as the text returns again to Andromache, then to its sequence of other exiles, finally to end in a gesture where meaning has become so generally dispersed that it is unnameable:

> Aux captifs, aux vaincus! . . . à bien d'autres encor!

A student reading French poetry for the first time once commented in class that this poem might have been "better" had it ended a few stanzas earlier. Other students agreed, and as discussion went on it became clear that the text as is had not provided the sense of an ending, the assertion of closure, they wanted from it. Instead of providing an ending, the poem merely stops, and that fall into silence, it became clear, frustrated their desire for a sense of stabilization, or for the stability of sense. This open ending, in which untold numbers of substitute possibilities are darkly evoked, was just not satisfying. I would suspect, though, that the feeling of disappointment or of being thwarted that my students had felt did not derive solely from the poem's last stanzas. The vague and general expectation of closure that one brings to any text is intensified in "Le Cygne" by its overt attempt to account for its origin, and the failure of that narrative account in the opening stanzas. Given an ambiguous, unclear, or undecidable opening, one might well wish all the more urgently for at least the satisfaction of a "good" ending.

It is tempting to claim that "Le Cygne" divides itself into two simple parts that might be labeled something like "before" and "after," or be given distinguishable identities, or be said to participate in contrastive processes. One might borrow from the language of psychoanalysis, for example, to call the two halves by the names of Condensation and Displacement. Such a reading would assert that the *cygne* arrives upon the text layered with meaning, as if the lightning it beseeches had struck it already in a moment prior to the text. Arriving, then, having already attained the stature of an emblem, symbol, or metaphor, in a second moment its privilege is undone by an endless metonymical chain. Or one might restrict oneself to the text's own generative metaphor of liquidity and speak in terms of "the containment of meanings" and the later *mise en question* of that possibility, as does Nathaniel Wing.[7] Then again, one might explore the political rather than the rhetorical force of the swan's instability as symbol and show how the passage from swan to *négresse* and beyond reflects a consciousness of an historically determined human situation. Edward J. Ahearn thus reads the slippage into the metonymic chain as the practice of an aesthetic that combats alienation:

the poem builds a sense of community for a world that denies
it, and in that way represents the highest function of art within
a degraded human context.[8]

Each of these readings, like my own, works to interpret the poem's
expansion, drift, or slippage away from its central and titulary figure. But care must be taken not to assume a greater degree of containment or innocence than the text in fact offers us in its opening
stanzas. The text does not quite enact for us a fall from stable sense
to the proliferation of sense, for example; rather, it comes into being
unaccountably to proffer an act in which sense is provisionally read
into the world through the mediation of a fiction. To put the matter
in more Baudelairean, less analogical terms, the poem acts out the
polarities of subjectivity that fascinated the poet—the "*centralisa-
tion*" and "*vaporisation*" of the self. If "Le Cygne" ends a bit more
loosely than a less literally understood denouement might lead us to
anticipate, it also begins as already somewhat undone.

My interest here is in exploring a textual practice by Baudelaire
that I call comicality—a practice that, among other things, imbues
the texts I'm discussing with a resistance to the very categories and
oppositions that they seem to call forth in order to be read. "Le
Cygne" interests me particularly at this point because, to the extent
that it is an "open-ended" text, it is open at both ends. It may not be
able to arrest the slippage from figure to figure once its figuration
gets underway, but neither is it able to account quite precisely for
how the process of figuration began in the first place. It has no
single first place, but rather emerges from an unreadable nexus in
order to read the world in a most provisional manner that fails in an
ontological sense, since a poem that drifts out and away from its
centralizing figure cannot at the same time claim the centrality we
traditionally demand of being. But if the poem cannot claim to be,
and can, inverting MacLeish, only claim to mean—and to challenge
in passing the fundamental distinction between meaning and being—
it nonetheless attains to an existence as poetic text. There is a certain
majestic bravado in this display of the precarious nature of the poetic quest for a meaningful equilibrium between self and world—a
bravado exemplified by Baudelaire's rude inclusion here of "bric-à-
brac" in the lexicon of French poetry. The poem inexplicably causes

a swan to become the sign of adequation between memory and actuality, between the literary past and the written present, and it then undoes the stability of that adequation as if the text itself were "rongé d'un désir sans trève." The swan is made to hover for an instant as the fulfillment of the desire that it ultimately can only reflect; then it recedes into an endless horizontal slippage, leaving behind it no more than the trace of that desire, which is the poem.

The Economic Problem of Allegory

That the world is *my* world, shows itself in the fact that the limits of language (*the* language which I understand) mean the limits of my world.
—Wittgenstein, *Tractatus* 5.62

J'aime les titres mystérieux ou les titres pétards.
—Letter to Poulet-Malassis

Set deeply within the poems of *Les Fleurs du Mal,* toward the end of the chapter called "Les Fleurs du Mal," in the position of the heraldic *mise-en-abyme,* is a text that responds to, or anticipates, the problems of allegorization posed by "Le Cygne." The poem's sole title is "Allégorie," and it invites us, as we shall see, to read it as a meditation on that title—not on the rhetorical device of allegory in general, but on *allégorie, symbole, emblème, image,* or *correspondance,* since Baudelaire makes no functional distinction among these terms.[9] The poem asks us: what is the site, or the sight, of the imagination as it seeks to interpret the world? As it goes about exploring its question, the poem will afford us both an illustration and a critique of an aesthetic centrality that will call into question the centrality of aesthetics. "Allégorie" may well be one of Baudelaire's earliest poems, while "Le Cygne" is no doubt one of his last verse texts; if the two works bridge the alleged maturation of the poet and, like the ace of hearts and the queen of spades of the first "Spleen," "causent sinistrement de leurs amours défunts," so much the better: obsessions are most noted for their durability.

Let me introduce this poem through a contrapuntal citation from the *Salon de 1859,* where Baudelaire writes about the imaginative faculty. The visible surfaces of the world, he says, offer themselves to us like goods in a store, to which we then assign value and proceed to consume:

> Tout l'univers visible n'est qu'un magasin d'images et de signes auxquels l'imagination donnera une place et une valeur relative; c'est une espèce de pâture que l'imagination doit digérer et transformer. (*O.C.,* II, 627)

The question I will pursue in reading "Allégorie," and one that the prose text does not consider, is that of the point (of view) from which the relativity of place and value becomes imaginable. The poem presents us with a beautiful woman in the most direct manner possible, discusses her visibility at some length, and relates her then to death. I will suggest here that this figure is not merely contained within the "magasin d'images" of the Baudelairean world, but is rather, in some sense, its proprietor. Here is the poem:

Allégorie

C'est une femme belle et de riche encolure,
Qui laisse dans son vin traîner sa chevelure.
Les griffes de l'amour, les poisons du tripot,
Tout glisse et tout s'émousse au granit de sa peau.
Elle rit à la mort et nargue la Débauche,
Ces monstres dont la main, qui toujours gratte et fauche,
Dans ses jeux destructeurs a pourtant respecté
De ce corps ferme et droit la rude majesté.
Elle marche en déesse et repose en sultane;
Elle a dans le plaisir la foi mahométane,
Et dans ses bras ouverts, que remplissent ses seins,
Elle appelle des yeux la race des humains.
Elle croit, elle sait, cette vierge inféconde
Et pourtant nécessaire à la marche du monde,
Que la beauté du corps est un sublime don

Qui de toute infamie arrache le pardon.
Elle ignore l'Enfer comme le Purgatoire,
Et quand l'heure viendra d'entrer dans la Nuit noire,
Elle regardera la face de la Mort,
Ainsi qu'un nouveau-né,—sans haine et sans remords.

(*O.C.,* I. 116)

This poem was first published in the 1857 *Fleurs du Mal,* although some version of it may date back to 1843.[10] A certain lack of formal dexterity, along with a generally "pagan" thematic, situate it no doubt with the texts of Baudelaire's youth. But it may be of interest precisely because it is an early poem that is rarely called upon to enforce critical arguments. That critical neglect may be due in part to the way "Allégorie" asserts the beauty of its subject without, however, quite grounding itself in the mode of representation. Consider the two first lines:

C'est une femme belle et de riche encolure,
Qui laisse dans son vin traîner sa chevelure.

This couplet cannot be said to evoke the beauty of its subject; rather, it seems to celebrate the poem's power to propose beauty without individualizing, illustrating, or concretizing it, as a portrait might. The procedure is radically different from the well-known portrayals of women that we find in "Sisina," "A une Mendiante rousse," or "A une Malabaraise." The capacity of language simply to put forth a possibility of beauty is underscored by the abstract referentiality of the proposition "c'est une. . . ." Beauty, in this case, is a plain assertion. That assertion is not merely proleptic, for nowhere in the poem will the woman be described. We are given, instead of a sense of what beauty is, only some sense of what it does.

Nor do we find in "Allégorie" another constitutive role in the genre of Baudelairean portraiture—a *je* in relation to whom the captivating power of the woman is explained. The beautiful woman who is presented without concrete detail is also isolated within the text, cut off from the *je-tu* relation of praise or seduction. She exists as a listing of attributes that is grammatically governed by the monotonous reiteration of *elle* as the subject of every principal clause in the text. The sole exception to that grammatical regularity occurs in line 4:

Tout glisse et tout s'émousse au granit de sa peau.

That line, emphasized as it is by breaking the governance of "elle," evokes an impenetrability that seems to extend to the relation between poet and subject. Nowhere else in Baudelaire can we find a woman presented with such a combination of distance and admiration. Eschewing the banal dynamic of seduction, the text works through mere induction, as if there were more to this lady than meets the I.

It is for that reason, perhaps, that Marcel Ruff never pauses to consider the poem as connected to the bodily presence of a woman, and reads it instead as an aesthetic statement. In *L'Esprit du mal et l'esthétique baudelairienne*, he construes the beautiful woman of "Allégorie" as a Parnassian sister of the strident speaker of "La Beauté":

Allégorie, qui montre dans la beauté du corps

. . . un sublime don
Qui de toute infamie arrache le pardon,

relève de Gautier et de la même esthétique qui a inspiré le sonnet de *La Beauté*. . . . Il est à présumer que ces vers ont été écrits au moment où Baudelaire se rapprochait le plus de l'Ecole Païenne et de l'art pour l'art.[11]

Ruff thus reads the poem as aligned with the figure of marmoreal beauty of "La Beauté," that resistant ideal of perfection who never laughs and never cries, and against whose unyielding breast feckless poets hurl themselves with lacerating results. Such a reading is astonishing, to say the least, given the opening couplet of "Allégorie." It is difficult to imagine an evocation of a less marmoreal quality: the poem begins with no more than a tempting hiss, proposing a beauty that is first dispersed among the semantic ambiguities of the "riche encolure," and then shifted to that most diaphanous of all possible parts of the body—the long strands of hair that drag, dip, sway, and soak in a glass of wine with a nonchalance that is suggestive to the extent that it shows a certain impropriety about this body, a sharing of it with other objects in the world. The "crinière lourde" of "La Chevelure" has a more stony quality than this diaspora of being in a vague interchange between hair and wine. It is this aspect of generosity, selflessness, or promiscuity that the phrase "riche encolure" reinforces, as Pichois implies in his notes. Baudelaire is either, he says, using "encolure" to denote the general appearance of the woman, or he is using a word most properly used to designate the neck or withers of an animal in relation to this feminine figure (*O.C.,* I, 1065–66). Or perhaps he is doing both, through a phrase that animalizes this beautiful woman in the same gesture that it sums up her power of self-presentation.

Beyond the opening couplet we do find, though, a claim to impenetrability in the next two lines, which culminate in the hemistich "au granit de sa peau." The fact that the now silent *t* of "granit" was still sounded in the mid-nineteenth century results in a hiatus of the breath that further stresses the inviolate border of the skin of the beautiful woman. No doubt the reader is led to recuperate this apparent contradiction by raising the second couplet to the level of moral statement, resolving the tension between the figure's animality and impenetrability by positing the second quality as a spiritual one, yielding the cliché of the noble, or distanced, and thus virtuous whore. Rather than engage in this shift of registers, let us for the moment simply acknowledge the play of antimonies in these four lines, where both volatile and marmoreal qualities are set into motion around the figure of the woman.

As we read on, this polarity is further complicated. The next lines follow from lines 3 and 4, in a highly stylized form of allegorization through personification; but if "la Mort" and "la Débauche" are defied, that defiance is accomplished through the verbs *rire* and *narguer,* which by no means imply the stony aloofness of the impassive figure of "La Beauté." Quite the contrary, in fact: mockery and teasing imply active and risky exchanges with their object, in a sequence of encounters and withdrawals—or poses. Throughout the text, the beautiful woman moves, poses, and assumes another pose, until at last she puts on a face against annihilation. This terminal pose confounds because of its vacuity: its power results from its lack. Unlike the shrill figure of "La Beauté," the beautiful woman is without a single stance, an essence, or a unique formal quality. Her essential trait lies in her mobility; her invulnerability seems to stem from her very fluidity. She exists only as a "femme belle," which is to say as a network of poses, fictions, attitudes, or attributes.

A critic who is concerned with establishing grounds for asserting a Baudelairean progress toward some form of moral or aesthetic *sagesse* will have to choose between the antimonies of this allegorical figure in order to privilege one set—the marmoreal, with Ruff, for example—over the other. He will, like the speaker of "Le Cygne," engage meaning as a function of desire, and will, in so doing, repeat the gesture that the comical element in these poems works to expose rather than extol. In the last analysis, it is only the eye of the poet, and his act of writing, that can resolve the antimony between the wine-soaked hair and the granite skin of this essentially formless *figura*. But how can essence be without form? How can beauty be attained through evanescence? What can be said for a pose whose essential trait lies in its easy availability to the eye? These questions are more directly raised by Baudelaire in his remarks on modernity, as in the essay on Constantin Guys. But they are strongly implicit in this early poem, despite the complete withdrawal of the lyrical *je* who might otherwise ask them. Instead, the speaking subject effaces itself, isolating the poem's figure in speechless vacuity and giving the text its sole but resonant title of "Allegory."

Because the "speaker" of the poem is most marked by his reluctance to enunciate his relation to the beautiful woman, and because she is in turn deprived of speech, there exists a double psychological gap in "Allégorie." The poem even achieves a certain mystery through its refusal to "go into depth": it seems content to praise the power of surfaces, but never labels them as superficial. The text is dominated by words that call attention to surfaces in their role as borders between inside and outside. The "beauty" of these surfaces seems to reside in their visibility as an interplay with the world— now winy hair, now stony skin; now an aloof pose, now a beckoning call from the eye. It is this very interplay of surface and depth that creates the demand for an understanding to which the poet responds—a demand that issues from his own eye and that finds itself already articulated in the labile borders of the woman. This play of projection/introjection between the eye and that body is sketched elsewhere at length, in Baudelaire's dedication of *Les Paradis artificiels,* and is addressed to the mysterious J. G. F.—a *jeune, gentille femme* has been one speculation.

A des esprits niais il paraîtra singulier, et même impertinent, qu'un tableau de voluptés artificielles soit dédié à une femme, source la plus ordinaire des voluptés les plus naturelles. Toutefois, il est evident que comme le monde naturel pénètre dans le spirituel, lui sert de pâture, et concourt ainsi à opérer cet amalgame indéfinissable que nous nommons notre individualité, la femme est l'être qui projette la plus grande ombre ou la plus grande lumière dans nos rêves. La femme est fatalement suggestive; elle vit d'une autre vie que la sienne propre; elle vit spirituellement dans les imaginations qu'elle hante et qu'elle féconde. (*O.C.,* I, 399)

Woman, in this passage, does not declare or explain but rather suggests, and apparently need not speak in order to do so: she has only to live, to exist, in order to penetrate and make fertile the mental life of the other. Or, to shift to the oral register of Baudelaire's tropology, her physical presence becomes a "fodder" which, properly digested, is the source of "spiritual" or mental or linguistic life.[12] Her privileged position as the greatest source of imaginative activity suggests a status of priority for woman: she is the beloved *milieu* from which scale, value, appearance, and dimension can be reckoned. Instead of being yet another influence on the imagination, she emerges in this passage as the very horizon of imaginative possibilities.

In a dense article called "Le Corps de Jeanne," Michel Deguy has already discussed the intensity with which Baudelaire's poetry continually returns to its gynocentric horizon. By means of this body a poetic language gauges the relation of self to otherness, seeing it now in its immensity ("La Géante"), as celestial analogon ("Je t'adore à l'égal de la voûte nocturne"), as driven martyr ("Une martyre"); now as rotting continuity ("Une charogne"), the threat of death

("Le Vampire"), or deprecation and humiliation ("La Béatrice"). Of woman in Baudelaire, Deguy writes: "Elle déploie l'*imagination* qui permet de voir, avec sa mesure; et elle est reprise, en tant que centre, par le dédoublement de la vue qu'elle opère, source de l'oxymore et prise dans l'oxymore."[13] It is the body of the woman—in the fascinating and memorialized play of its surfaces—that haunts the imagination; it is the ghost that allows the poet the powerful and primary likenings that open the world as dwelling for poetry.

The beautiful woman of "Allégorie" does not, I would suggest, exist as the allegory of some corresponding sense: she is not the vehicle that carries us off toward its tenor on a one-way voyage to meaning. She exists instead, beneath the ponderous title of the poem, as the threshold of allegorization—as the nonself by which the self comes to gauge itself in an arena of visibility that she opens. Critics have sometimes read her, out of the necessity of reading her into a network of correspondences, as an allegorical representation of Prostitution. In order to do so, they have capitalized on the mention of her sterile necessity in the most clichéd manner possible, recuperating her as a participant in the "world's oldest profession." That reading requires a leap not only across the poem's title, which might as easily name its subject as its genre, but over the problematic referentiality of the notion "prostitution" in Baudelaire: he, after all, does apply that word to describe the activity of the artist in one of the most cited entries of *Fusées*: "Qu'est-ce que l'art? Prostitution" (*O.C.,* I, 649). The poet's assimilation of art to prostitution should demand that any "allegorical" reading of this text be carried beyond the level of cliché toward one where it might be a question of artistic activity. At that level, the poem tends to become an allegory of allegory. It begins to seem as if this beautiful woman, instead of selling access to herself, were rather selling only tickets to a match taking place in an arena or theater where she is more the director than a participant in the program. The shifting set of borders that simultaneously comprise the woman as other and that are appropriated through the desiring eye as "mine" inaugurate the site of allegory, where it is a question of the relation between the isolated eye and all that circumfuses it.

To the extent that we might claim allegorization as the poem's topic, the mysterious woman with neither essence nor psychology seems to figure nothing more or less than what Deguy calls "contiguity":

> La "contiguïté" essentielle n'est pas spatiale au sens objectif de ce qui voisine effectivement pour la perception. C'est la *métaphore* (ou *comparaison* entendue comme . . . champ et modes de comparution), pour une vaste mesure, toujours la même, ouverte au regard poétique, née en même temps que le désir reconnaissant "son" corps, qui dispose la "distance," c'est-à-dire en même temps l'un pour et par l'autre le proche et le lointain, la possibilité de cette dimension que les choses soient toutes aussi proches aussi éloignées les unes des autres que les unes des autres, et ainsi de commencer le jeu des métonymies ou poème, qui litanise "l'union libre." Ce mien corps de la femme laisse tout se rapprocher, permet les "rapprochements," et les étoiles être dans cette proximité ou distance première. (335)

Deguy's insight into the function of woman in other Baudelairean texts helps us understand the poem's claim that the beautiful woman is both unproductive, "inféconde," and yet necessary to the working, "la marche," of the world. She is not a means of production herself: she does not call a world into existence; indeed nothing issues forth from her. But she exists as the threshold across which things emerge for themselves, *like* her. This virgin, forever intact through her position in otherness, is the fold of representability, the space of the *comme* in assimilation, the possibility of as well as the irreducible gap within "identification." "Contiguity" tries to name— and Baudelaire's woman to figure—the origin of imagination, the space of the hymen as both proximity and veiling, from which language can represent the world in its approximation.[14]

The title functions, then, to make the text beneath it appear to the reader as imbued with a demand similar to the demand that the world exerts upon the poet, as he is described in a letter of 1865:

> *L'homme raisonnable* n'a pas attendu que Fourier vînt sur la terre pour comprendre que la Nature est un *verbe,* une allégorie, un moule, un repoussé, si vous voulez.[15]

Though the title "Allégorie" surfaces as a noun, it imposes on the reader the force of an imperative, demanding that the world offer a principle through which it might become a universe or cosmos. The text beneath it takes on the qualities of that *repoussé*, if you wish. If you wish nature to be embossed with raised designs that connote significance; if you desire significance in nature, or in woman, as nature's most powerful representation of itself to you. The relation between desire and the sense of the world cannot be underestimated here, nor can the role of raised signs—the embossing of the significant upon the natural that causes Baudelaire to call the world a "repoussé."

If the body of the beautiful woman, in its endless display of poses, its degrees of texture, its gazes and gestures, figures a *milieu* through which the world can appear in its human dimension, that same body, as the text proffers it, offers as its center and in the poem's central lines a double *repoussé*, or a burgeoning of senses:

> Et dans ses bras ouverts, que remplissent ses seins,
> Elle appelle des yeux la race des humains.

At the center of the text, the figure of the woman beckons us toward its center—her *seins* or her *sein*, the French equivalent of such comforting notions as "breast," "heart," "hearth," and "home." But the text takes care not to overlook the doubleness of the body's center, maintaining the plural form of the noun whose sense becomes so elastic in that language. In "Le Corps de Jeanne," Deguy discusses at length the way in which the breast becomes a fantasmatically powerful *repoussé* in the figurality of French as an overdetermined surface that proposes a *coeur* as a hidden inside—an intimate center of the living body, or the *sein* of the self. The two words then come to act as synonyms in various figures of speech, as in for example "au sein (coeur) de la famille," or "au coeur (sein) de la ville." Or in "Le Balcon," where Baudelaire deploys them as an interchangeable pair of signifiers:

> Que ton sein m'était doux! que ton coeur m'était bon!

The problematic way in which the sign system of *sein* and *coeur* fail to produce a localizable interior signified, but rather establish a system of interchangeability, inscribes itself in the twin breasts of the beckoning woman of "Allégorie." We are being called "home" to an "originary synonomy," as Deguy calls it: "Le sein est le sein des seins: au coeur du corps le sein; au sein du corps le coeur" (341). Whether we view the choice as a paradigmatic one, calling us to choose between breasts, or as a syntagmatic one that focuses on the priority of breast or heart, we are trapped in this play of synonomy and desire. The moral, central sense of a center finds itself in a relation of perpetual exchange, since the moral sense of whichever object we elevate to a centralized status will always be on loan from the defigured other. At the "heart" of the problem, the distinction between vehicle and tenor is called into question, as Deguy notes:

> Nous sommes à un foyer des figures, au foyer de la figuration, où le corps est bien le figuratif; sans pouvoir décider de l'antériorité, ni préséance, de l'une sur l'autre; remarquant bien qu'en tout état de cause la *métonymie* (de la partie sein pour tout le corps) n'a lieu, n'est privilégiée que pour autant qu'elle s'adosse à ce foyer des figures—d'ou se monnayeront toutes les *allégories* qu'on voudra. (341)

The "foyer" in question locates itself in that zone of the body where *sein* and *coeur* exist in physical proximity—in a "metonymical" relation to each other—while at the same time asserting themselves in a privileged relation of intimate centrality and sense—always and each time at the expense of the other term. The primordial system of *sein* and *coeur* is then situated at an axis where the priority and value of metaphor and metonymy, in relation to each other, become indistinguishable. And "Allégorie" displays at its center a centrality that is always doubled against itself—either "literally" or "figuratively"—where sense slides, from either *sein* to *sein,* or from *sein* to *coeur,* across surfaces, unable to anchor itself firmly in an allegorical sense to be found beneath the *repoussé* of appearance. At the center of the text is the center of the body of a beautiful woman; but that center is at heart a system of slippage rather than a home for a sense or a soul beneath a surface. And if this figure defies the power of annihilation at the end of the poem, it is because nothing has taken place where she dwells: the *milieu* that she is does not, itself, participate in the process of life that death overwhelms; instead it stands at, or as, its border. As a "foyer de figures," an axis at which metaphor and metonymy lose their distinguishing traits, the beautiful woman is the enabler of certain "transports des sens" that vitalize existence, but she is never their *telos,* destination, or home. The final line of the poem makes clear that she never escapes the limits of the newborn, existing instead on the thresholds of language and of any narrative quantum of time. The text withdraws its figure from narrativity and death, by displaying her existence beyond and before narration.

Baudelaire was fond of citing Stendhal's comment that beauty consists in the promise of happiness. He seems to have taken it to mean not that beauty entailed any pact or vow but that it merely sets a certain happiness forth in the world, as the transcendence of any given present. In the poem we are reading, the title of "Allégorie" sets the beautiful woman of its text into circulation as the promise of sense. But we find that the text does not exactly keep the promise it proposes but rather explores the performative conditions of the promise itself. Instead of fulfilling its promise, "Allégorie" shows how sense slides along surfaces of interchanging meaning in an attempt to read a *repoussé* whose depth or center cannot be localized, trivialized, or ultimately allegorized. If "Allégorie" suffers from an economic problem similar to the one that Freud proposed for masochism, then that problem lies in the tension between a closed economy of "symbolic" sense promised by a generic reading of its title and an open, decentered economy of sense that the text articulates beneath a title that seems less to name the poem's modality than to name the subject of its meditation.

Objects of Knowledge

> Le goût précoce de femmes. Je confondais
> l'odeur de la fourrure avec l'odeur de la
> femme. Je me souviens. . . .
> —*Fusées*

The lines of "Allégorie" that have led some readers to see the poem
as about Prostitution, and which lead me to read the beautiful
woman as a figure of contiguity, form the first half of a single sentence, which runs:

> Elle croit, elle sait, cette vierge inféconde,
> Et pourtant nécessaire à la marche du monde,
> Que la beauté du corps est un sublime don
> Qui de toute infamie arrache le pardon.

This is the only psychological claim the text makes with regard to
the beautiful woman, and the proof texts for *Les Fleurs du Mal* show
the poet trying out several possibilities of positioning himself in relation to her belief in beauty. In one version he opens the sentence
with a negated question in the conditional mood, implying an at
least skeptical distanciation from her:

> Ne croirait-elle pas, cette vierge inféconde . . . ?

Then he tries merely to isolate her in an indicative statement of
her belief:

> Elle seule, elle croit, cette vierge inféconde. . . .

Ultimately, however, he eliminates the implication that her belief is
eccentric, and affirms it not merely as belief but as knowledge itself:

> Elle croit, elle sait, cette vierge inféconde. . . .

It is as if the writerly gestures of denegation disappear in the corrections, as if the distance taken from the figure lessens to the point
where some sort of solidarity is established between poet and
woman. She no longer simply believes something about beauty; she
knows, and the poet claims to know that she knows.

Both the beautiful woman and the poet seem to know that beauty
has the power to exact forgiveness—that its power is bound up with
ethical force. They know that beauty sublimely elevates its embodiment to the level of some moral justification. Exactly what such a

claim might mean in the context of not only the poem, but the *Fleurs du Mal* in general, remains now to be discussed. That claim echoes— like "de longs échos"—Kant's notion of beauty as the symbol of morality, which provided the philosopher with the title of his penultimate paragraph in the "Critique of Aesthetical Judgment." But this echo is not a mere sonorous repetition: more like the echo of Echo, it is a partial repetition that serves to dramatize difference rather than reduplicate the same.

We have seen that the essence of the beautiful woman consists in her shifty nonessentiality, her poses and peripheral exchanges with the world. Her beauty resides in her volatile availability to the eye and the imagination in its quest for a world on a poetic scale. This beauty is not exactly formless, for it takes on shapes and attitudes; but it is form-free in that it is multiform, labile, and evanescent. The Form of this beauty is always a pose. To align the figure of this woman with an ethical claim for beauty deriving from Kant and popularized in France by Victor Cousin amounts to an informaliza- tion of Beauty, a calling into question of the status of the Form, and a simultaneous, sedimented naming of the beautiful as that which informs, makes representable, despite its mutability.[16] If this infor- malization is couched in the theological terminology of *don, infamie,* and *pardon,* it is not by chance, for the formality of beauty is the linchpin in the Kantian argument that the Beautiful is the analagon of the Good, as we shall see. Any informalization of beauty must engage a philosophical tradition that would put Beauty in the service of philosophy as the "symbol," as Kant calls it, of the Good. At stake in this informalization is the restoration of beauty to the senses, to the animate, and to the "fleuve de la vitalité" that Baudelaire ad- mires as the object of Guys' sketches (*O.C.,* II, 692). These stakes are high, and well beyond the passions of a youthful enthusiasm for the doctrine of "l'Art pour l'Art."

Let us briefly review how the formality of the beautiful—as op- posed to the awesome formlessness of the contradistinctive category of the sublime—comes to play a key role in the system of Kant's thinking. The introduction to the third *Critique* states clearly that the process of thinking through the two prior *Critiques* has resulted in a philosophical impasse. By dividing human experience as they have, the *Critiques* of pure and practical reason have become monumental edifices of thought, but between the realms that they treat respectively, a huge gap now threatens. Kant calls it

> the great gulf that separates the supersensible from phenomena. The concept of freedom determines nothing in respect to the theoretical cognition of nature, and the natural concept determines nothing in respect to the practical laws of freedom.[17]

The difficulty that Kant is describing here, and that he will try to resolve in the third *Critique,* arises from the vividness with which the two others have shown that the self and the world are experienced in radically different ways. As Kant has it:

> That they do not constitute *one* realm arises from this that the natural concept represents its objects in intuition, not as things in themselves, but as mere phenomena; the concept of freedom, on the other hand, represents in its object a thing in itself, but not an intuition. (11)

If an irreducible gap lies between self and world, or freedom and nature, then the world of phenomena is forever veiled by a shade of absurdity: phenomena are doomed to appear to consciousness as gratuitous, and their reason for being, to appear inaccessible. It is against this disharmony between the two realms—against absurdity, whose etymological sense meant dissonance—and in the name of a harmonious relation between self and world that Kant will deploy the legislative desire of philosophical discourse. His project necessitates a definition of beauty that will enable Beauty to constitute the subjective experience that transcends private subjectivity without recourse to the laws of sensational empiricism. Beauty, thus defined, will emerge as the conceptual bridge across the threatening abyss. Whence the strictures imposed by its definition:

> In the case of an object whose form (not the matter of its representation or sensation), in the mere reflection upon it (without reference to any concept to be obtained of it), is judged as the ground of a pleasure in the representation of such an object, this pleasure is judged as bound up with the representa-

tion necessarily, and, consequently, not only for the subject which apprehends this form, but for every judging being in general. The object is then called beautiful. (27)

As the perception of beautiful form, the experience of the beautiful neither resides completely within the subject nor within the object, and for that capital reason implies its potentially universal communicability between subjects. The experience of beauty involves pleasure because it entails the revelation of universal forms of mind by means of corresponding formal properties in beautiful objects. The formality of beauty, by overriding the individual peculiarities of sensuous pleasure, allows for the proposal of a universal harmony that aligns freedom with nature, and purpose with law. Beauty's formal property allows it to appear as purposive, or bound toward some apparent but unknowable purpose. It allows the I-am-bound-towards of self-sense to be recognized within a world perceived as a harmonious fellow that exists as-if-bound-towards. The key to that fellowship is the beautiful object, in which purpose, or self-sense, sees itself reflected in the endless purposiveness of the beautiful. Because the apprehension of beauty is both subjective and universal, the isolated subject can experience the world as a potentially harmonious set of phenomena—in potential harmony with his own and others' finite sense of purpose.

The formality of beauty provides the basis for the claim that it can attain to a universal assent, which ultimately allows Kant to propose the beautiful as the symbol of the morally good. Because Beauty resides in Form, it is susceptible of universal apprehension. The harmony that Beauty generates between Kant's faculties of mind does more, then, than allow the world to appear as purposive; it sings of the possible edification of all humans, united by means of the pleasure of so "pure a satisfaction":

By this the mind is made conscious of a certain ennoblement and elevation above the mere sensibility to pleasure received through sense, and the worth of others is estimated in accordance with a like maxim of their judgment. . . . Taste makes possible the transition, without any violent leap, from the charm of sense to habitual moral interest, as it represents the imagination in its freedom as capable of purposive determination for the understanding, and so teaches us to find even in objects of sense a free satisfaction apart from any charm of sense. (199–200)

The freedom of Beauty's satisfaction is guaranteed by its formality— its being "apart from any charm of sense"—which in turn guarantees the linking of subject to subject, as humanity, and subject to world, in harmony.

Kant's titular claim in paragraph 59, that Beauty is the symbol of Morality, is followed by an inquiry into what it means to be a symbol, in his sense. At this point in his argument, we find him entertaining a question that is both ancient and evergreen: how can (re)presentation, *Darstellung*, be brought into play in order to make real concepts that are not in themselves to be found in the world? How can Beauty be said to symbolize Morality—or, what is the modality of symbolization that can be said to obtain in such a claim? It is at this point that the philosopher's problem most closely resembles that of the poet of "Allégorie," for both are concerned with the ground upon which might be established a link between moral imperative and sensible phenomena. Baudelaire's observation that poetry must, and can only, be "involontairement philosophique" rings true at this juncture in Kant's discussion (*O.C.,* II, 9). On the other hand, it is curious to find that Kant—this most discursive of philosophers, who has extolled poetry as the primary and exemplary art form—is compelled to stress that the symbolization in question partakes of a cognitive mode that lies wholly outside of discourse. As he writes in a footnote: "The intuitive in cognition must be opposed to the discursive (not to the symbolical)" (197).

The symbolical, that is, can exist outside, and opposed to, the discursive, opening itself to immediate intuition, without need of words to establish its apprehension. The crucial symbols in question do not participate in a process of signification; they are:

not mere *characterizations* or designations of concepts by accompanying sensible signs which contain nothing belonging to the intuition of the object and only serve as a means for reproducing the concepts, according to the law of association of the imagination, and consequently in a subjective point of view. These are words or visible (algebraical, even mimetical) signs, as mere expressions for concepts. (197)

The symbol is not a mediated sign, but rather what Kant calls an "analogy"

in which the judgment exercises a double function, first applying the concept to the object of a sensible intuition, and then applying the mere rule of reflection made upon that intuition to a quite different object of which the first is only a symbol. (197–98)

Beauty can thus be said to symbolize the morally good, not because the good and the beautiful share certain sense properties, but because beauty pleases the reflective judgment in a manner similar to the pleasure of the good. This "symbol," whose similarity to something other than itself resides outside any principle of perceptual resemblance, sounds something like the vehicle in the conceits of the metaphysical poets—as, for example, Donne's likening of a compass to two parting lovers. But Kant's analogy absolutely transcends all linguistic mediation: it is an apodictic analogy beyond "sensible signs."

If on the one hand this analogical principle of symbolization transcends the materiality of the sensible signifier, it seems to work, on the other hand, like language, and when Kant goes on to offer examples of analogies, it is to language that he returns:

Our language is full of indirect presentations of this sort, in which the expression does not contain the proper schema for the concept, but merely a symbol for reflection. . . . [These are] not schematical but symbolical hypotheses and expressions for concepts, not by means of a direct intuition, but only by analogy with it, *i.e.* by the transference of reflection upon an object of intuition to a quite different concept to which perhaps an intuition can never directly correspond. (198)

The transference that takes place here seems similar to the crossing performed through rhetorical metaphor, but operates in a purer, transparent mode of cognition. Language provides merely the analogy of the "analogy": it is *like* the extradiscursive likening in question. It is, in other words, both the enabling and repressed structure that allows a juridical order in which the judgment can "give the law to itself in respect of the objects of so pure a satisfaction" (199).[18]

"In this supersensible ground," Kant says ("ground" being one of the words that he offers, not coincidentally, as "analogies"), the mind apprehends that the beautiful is like the morally good, without the mediation of discourse. The judgment, in a paradoxical formulation, is said to give itself the gift of this law. The difficulty in thinking the kind of exchange that is taking place here results from the strenuous closure that the philosopher is imposing upon the system of giving. Language is the model to be repressed, the source of the analogon, which can only be offered as an inferior example and then withdrawn from the supersensible circuit of exchange. Yet it is language that gives, by analogy, the model for the gift giving: it is language that allows, by virtue of its unmotivated, shifty quality, the demonstration of "transference of reflection upon an object of intuition to a quite different concept to which perhaps intuition can never directly correspond." The capacity of the "symbol" to give an intuition occurs both in accord with the rule of rhetoric and yet uncannily beyond the domain of the merely linguistic. The realm of language must be denied in order to prove the lawfulness of beauty as the symbol of the morally good.

It is the material aspect of language—its existence as the mediating "sensible sign"—that Kant must repress on his way toward the idealization of beauty as pure form, the immediately intuitable, the supersensible cognition of immaculate good. The mark of the insistent need to escape materiality can be read in his deployment of the rarefied term "hypotyposis" (derived from Greek) as the mental function from which symbolization obtains its operational power to intuit "presentations." In making his case for the existence of such hypotyposes, he offers the word twice in paragraph 59, each time following it with the parenthetical support of the German *Darstellung,* and then with a Latin amplification—first *subjectio sub adspectum,* then *exhibitiones*. The German noun, then the supplementary Latin phrases, occur as if to elevate and secure the notion of "hypotyposis," safeguarding it from the material sense of its Greek etymology: the word derives from *hypotypoein*, "to sketch, to make a pattern," and further from *tipos*, "impression, form, or type." It is as if the German and Latin support systems might serve to veil the trace of the material imprint, the stylus of writing, the palimpsestic shadow of print, that inhabit the formidable classical term. The implication of hypotyposis in the sensible, material stratum constitutes a residue of what Kant calls mere "characterization," and what we might call the foregrounding of the signifier.

Seamlessness and Discontinuity

> . . . cette gorge aiguë
> Qui n'a jamais emprisonné de coeur.
> –"Le Léthé"

An abiding concern for the materiality of language—its sedimented echoes, its location of sense in the Other, its availability to plays of meaning through sound, its resonance within the cultural text that delimits each human subjectivity—is a hallmark of our age as surely as a hostility to the inexactitude of naming marked the end of the seventeenth century, or the desire to transcend the mediation of language marked the work of a Kant or a Coleridge. Throughout this essay I have been asking how one might accurately situate *Les Fleurs du Mal* in relation to this materiality that resists a universalizing aesthetic program. Even so youthful a poem as "Allégorie" appears, at least by 1857, as a skillfully direct meditation on the workings of beauty. We find that the beautiful woman of the text functions to reveal herself as the possibility of valuation: she is the embodiment of appearance, the site where a poetic desire operates to envision the world in, and as, a proximate other.

This beauty appears as always embodied, and in the various modalities of the body, whether as near or far, elevating or repugnant, grandiose or trivial. It is subject to the vagrancies of matter, and for that reason it serves to adumbrate only possibilities or fictions. Beauty, for Baudelaire, partakes of a certain universality, but in a way distinct from the legislative function of beauty in Kant. For the philosopher, beauty contains its form by virtue of its potential to be hypostatized and abstracted to the level of supersensible form. For the poet, beauty does not precipitate form, but is rather the precipitate of desire. Its universality lies in its function as the threshold from which the existence of a universe opens itself to the imagination. In its formless plurality of poses, it lends itself to a spectrum of values, proportions, and distances—all in relation to a "me" that does not participate in the opacity of my own body but which arises before it as if to be the point from which my desire can be articulated as meaning. The beautiful woman of "Allégorie" "knows" that her surfaces are the text that responds to the allegorical imperative articulated through the title of the poem.

Les Fleurs du Mal deploys language, I would claim, in the essence of its fascinating materiality to create texts that mark themselves as fictions, or functions of desire rather than of cognition. That marking of the poem as construct is what I would call the comical practice of Baudelaire's verse. By means of a plurality of devices, a poem is inscribed impurely, tracing the gap between desire and fulfillment that inheres structurally in the desiring subject. Even if we look closely at a poem whose form and content seem at first to coalesce, we will find the trace of the comical; even if we turn to a formal exercise in harmony, we will find a dissonant echo in the linguistic register:

Harmonie du Soir

Voici venir les temps où vibrant sur sa tige
Chaque fleur s'évapore ainsi qu'un encensoir;
Les sons et les parfums tournent dans l'air du soir;
Valse mélancolique et langoureux vertige!

Chaque fleur s'évapore ainsi qu'un encensoir;
Le violon frémit comme un coeur qu'on afflige;
Valse mélancolique et langoureux vertige!
Le ciel est triste et beau comme un grand reposoir.

> Le violon frémit comme un coeur qu'on afflige,
> Un coeur tendre, qui hait le néant vaste et noir!
> Le ciel est triste et beau comme un grand reposoir;
> Le soleil s'est noyé dans son sang qui se fige.
>
> Un coeur tendre, qui hait le néant vaste et noir,
> Du passé lumineux recueille tout vestige!
> Le soleil s'est noyé dans son sang qui se fige . . .
> Ton souvenir en moi luit comme un ostensoir!
>
> (*O.C.*,I, 47)

This poem enacts a certain triumph: its virtuoso adaptation of the *pantoum* proclaims, by virtue of the repetition demanded by the form, a victory of memory over linear time which is enabled by a kind of ritual. The incantatory power of repeated lines on a two-rhyme scheme, alternating between the tense production of "-ige" and the lax openness of "-oir," seems to evoke the brittle sense of loss that time imposes on the speaker and the attenuation of that sense through the cultivation of the recuperative force of memory. More often than not, the lax rhyme is occasioned by likening elements in the speaker's present to the paraphernalia used in celebrating the Corpus Christi procession, as if to affirm the power of a private ritual to overcome, like the Christian festival, the power of time and death. The text, like the festival, celebrates the miraculous victory of the human aspiration to endure over the absurd entropy of the life process.

The poem celebrates, in other words, the power of repetition. Repetition, when employed as a formal—or theological—principle, can re-present the absent, overcome loss, and impose a sentimental order upon the intransigence of time. But in the very act of repeating itself, in the very gesture that lends it an hypnotic effect, the poem inscribes differences within repetition, as if to suggest that the coherent memory of the addressee is determined by the desire of the speaker, and that the stabilization of the *destinataire* functions reciprocally to generate a sense of identity for the poem's speaker. The inscription of difference is not accomplished through a lexical or morphemic change, which would eliminate the element of repetition, but rather by a syntactical change in the function of a repeated segment. The initial offering of "Un coeur tendre, qui hait le néant vaste et noir" occurs as an amplification of "un coeur qu'on afflige"; when the segment is repeated, though, it has become the subject of a verb phrase in the final stanza, and the exclamation point that initially closes the segment is displaced to the end of the following line. Because no more than syntax changes, the segment is allowed to recur triumphantly in the final stanza as part of the poem's climactic thematization. But the syntax has indeed shifted, undermining the victory of ritual over time, of memory over change, and opening the text to skeptical readings that might explore the ways in which the system of likenesses that the poem celebrates—between repeated segments, between private and public ritual objects, and between subjective identities over time—has been invaded from within by an insertion of difference.

It is the tendency to this self-invasion that I have been calling the comical practice of Baudelaire's verse. It is not so much a matter of a dialogue between texts of the kind that De Man delineates in the case of "Correspondances" and "Obsession," but rather of a dialogue never quite hushed and resolved within a text, problematizing simultaneously the very motion of "within" as the refuge where meaning takes its place. The dialogue might arise through the process of revising a poem, as it does in "Un Voyage à Cythère," or through the resonant contradiction in a phrase like "décor suborneur," whose overwrought deprecation of the mask causes it simultaneously to echo the gilded syllable of "or," sending the reader to the history of the words to explore that contradiction. Or dialogue might be the original principle that structures a poem like "Le Cygne," whose denouement is more an unraveling of plenitude than a satisfaction of readers' expectations. Or again, it might be overheard in the ambiguity of a title like "Allégorie," whose textual body can be read as a meditation on the relation of bodies to sense. Or it might assert itself through a whisper that calls into question the formal principle of a text like "Harmonie du Soir," insisting that the principle that formalizes the text derives more from a certain *volo* than from a *cogito*. And if I use here the term "dialogue" to characterize this self-invasion, I do so only heuristically; for how can the number of voices at play in these cases be delimited to merely a pair? A conversation generates these texts, and the subject of it is poetic impurity. How can one sign a name to a conversation? Only tentatively, and without a smile, at best.

Epilogue

I have tried to show that the verse poems of Baudelaire operate by playing off against each other two radically different attitudes toward the potentiality of poetic language. These poems do not contradict the traditional notion that the poetic project employs language as the transparent witness to moments when the interpreting poet and the interpretability of the world reflect each other in a stable, meaningful reciprocity; in fact they ground themselves in that tradition, bringing into play the reader's similar desire that the world offer itself to sense in the same gesture that it offers itself to the senses. Yet the poems I have dealt with engage a profound suspicion that the writing subject can never coincide with its transcription of a "moment of being"; that is, it can never achieve the language of immediate and full sense to which it aspires. What I have named the comical element in Baudelaire's verse resides in the irresolvable tension between poetic aspiration and suspicion. The poet's profoundly ambivalent attitude toward the possibilities of language produces texts that resist being located under the simple sign of either irony or sincerity, for these poems exist Otherwise, and suggest that it is only by submitting to the desire for a fantasmatic control over language that the poet can come to know the extent to which the self is fragmented in its quest for a specular stabilization of the world in meaning.

The poems I have discussed here are all carefully wrought monuments to a poetic desire that the poet understands to be structurally insatiable. They suggest that the quest for interpretations of the world as representations of the self's identity can at best result in an evanescent fiction whose metaphorical plenitude is always by nature overfull and spilling into serial substitution. The poet is, by definition, he who longs to produce a text whose language will reflect the mending of the rift that language itself has opened in the subject; and he explores this longing as an original motive for poetry. His exploration consists neither in the assertion of poetic mastery, nor in the ironic deflation of mastery, but rather in inscribing his excentric relation to language within the poetic text. It is this project of inscription that Baudelaire calls, in the essay on laughter, the curious and noteworthy "introduction de cet élément insaisissable du beau jusque dans les oeuvres destinées à représenter à l'homme sa propre laideur. . . ."

There is no cause to believe that the poems with which I have dealt are especially idiosyncratic, although the textual practice that I call the comical cannot be disclosed without detailed attention to any given text in which it might occur. But it goes against the spirit of the inscription that I see at work in these texts simply to list, or rapidly suggest, other poems that share in the practice of the comical. Rather than attempt such an inventory, I wish instead to point out how we can read, in the light of the foregoing discussion, a Baudelairean self-portrait as an evocation of the comical poetic stance. The self-portrait is given in "Le Soleil" and is, as Benjamin observed, "probably the only place in *Les Fleurs du Mal* where Baudelaire is shown at his poetic labors."[1] In the poem, Baudelaire offers us a picture of the poet who goes about the urban, industrial, modern world in search of those occasions that might give rise to poetry. He describes the poetic quest as a "fantasque escrime," and I wish to note briefly the components of that fencing game.

The poet of "Le Soleil" is up with the sun, out to see what he can see and to see what he can say. But although his activity might depend on the visibility of things that the sun makes possible, it is not presented in any way as similar to the natural flow of light from the sun; instead, poetic activity resembles more a strange kind of shadowboxing that occurs in halting fits and starts:

> Je vais m'exercer seul à ma fantasque escrime,
> Flairant dans tous les coins les hasards de la rime,
> Trébuchant sur les mots comme sur les pavés,
> Heurtant parfois des vers depuis longtemps rêvés.
>
> (*O.C.,* I, 83)

The initial hemistich makes clear that the poet is accompanied, in his solitary enterprise, only by a representation of the poetic self— the *m'* that stands for the place of the self in his language. The abbreviated *m'* stands, that is, both for the pronoun *me* and for the *muse,* who is the figure of poetic language endowed with the power of reflecting back to the self the image of the Poet. The *m(us)e* that is the object in the pronominal verbal play announces a self-configuration as Poet: the speaker and his muse set forth together to engage the world in a duel whose goal is to transform the visible

into poetic discourse. We are left to wonder whether the imaginary
rival in this duel is the "outside" world that the poet encounters, or
whether it is the mirror image of the self as Poet. The idea of self-
fencing slips toward that of self-enclosure; but the rest of the stanza
resists such wordplay.

In the encounter between poet and world, it is the partnership of
the self and language that ends up by being called into question.
Language, at first perhaps assumed to be on the side of the poet in
this duel, begins to assume a material exteriority, and to resemble
the imaginary adversary. We see the poet's attention engaged in the
same random and sudden way that the foot might stumble over a
paving stone; and the words that might be thought to enhance ar-
resting moments of contact with the world are encountered instead
as accidental arrivals from some exterior source. Instead of asserting
that the poet exercises a mastery of language in the cause of an expressive recounting of his engagement with the world, the poem
names from the start two ways in which the pellucidity of poetic
consciousness is undermined by the very medium of its expression.

First, the materiality of language works to inject the element
of chance—"les hasards"—in the project of verse—"la rime."
Rhyming denotes the conventionality of verse poetry itself, against
which language offers a specific resistance. Moreover, the phrase
"les hasards de la rime" suggests that words may align themselves
in the poetic consciousness by virtue of their mere phonic properties—working like *correspondances,* but on a simply horizontal plane,
conjoined only by the material traits of the signifier. Second, the
above lines end with a display of the poetic project as the experience
of a temporal fragmentation of meaning. In his quest to transform
experience into sense, the poet finds his language emerging from an
unconscious past as the uncanny future meaning of the lived moment. We can follow the logic of the fourth line only by admitting
its power to problematize the self-containment of any present and
the self-governance of consciousness in its discovery of "meaning."
The poetic self that is displayed in the "fantasque escrime" of "Le
Soleil" ends up being interpreted by the world that it seeks to
interpret.

"Le Soleil" is an early poem, but Baudelaire took care to place it
strategically in the two editions of his verse whose publication he

lived to oversee. In both editions it functions as a signal text, appearing as the second poem of "Spleen et Idéal" in the 1857 edition, and then later as the second poem in the newly created sequence called "Tableaux Parisiens." In both cases, the poem, in its liminal position in relation to the most important thematic grouping of texts, shows a poet achieving distinction, not as he who tames the world through his mastery of language, but rather as he who undergoes a primordial submission to the material determination of both language and subjectivity. The poem underwrites its own project as the perpetual effort to maintain a precarious balance in the face of the material force of the world. It is this risky performance, put forth on the level of representation in "Le Soleil," but inscribed throughout Baudelaire's verse, that I have tried to elucidate.

Appendix

PROTOTEXT: VOYAGE A CYTHERE

> Le point de départ de cette pièce est
> quelques lignes de Gérard (*Artiste*) qu'il
> serait bon de retrouver.

Mon coeur comme un oiseau s'envolait tout joyeux,
Et planait librement à l'entour des cordages.
Le navire roulait sous un ciel sans nuages,
Comme un oiseau qu'enivre un soleil radieux.

5   Quelle est cette île triste et noire? C'est Cythère,
Me dit-on. Un pays fameux dans les chansons,
Eldorado banal de tous les vieux garçons.
Regardez, après tout, c'est une pauvre terre.

Ile des doux secrets et des fêtes du coeur,
10   De l'antique Vénus le superbe fantôme
Au-dessus de tes mers plane comme un arôme,
Et charge les esprits d'amour et de langueur.

Belle île aux myrtes verts, pleine de fleurs écloses,
Vénérée à jamais par toute nation,
15   Où les coeurs mortels en adoration
Font l'effet de l'encens sur un jardin de roses,

Ou du roucoulement éternel d'un ramier.
Cythère n'était plus qu'un terrain des plus maigres,
Un désert rocailleux troublé par des cris aigres.
20   J'entrevoyais pourtant un objet singulier.

Ce n'était pas un temple aux ombres bocagères,
Où la jeune prêtresse errant parmi les fleurs

Allait, le corps brûlé de secrètes chaleurs,
Entre-baîllant sa robe à des brises légères.

25   Mais voilà qu'en rasant la côte d'assez près
Pour troubler les oiseaux avec nos voiles blanches
Nous vîmes que c'était un gibet à trois branches
Du ciel se détachant en noir comme un cyprès.

De féroces oiseaux perchés sur leur pâture
30   Dévoraient avec rage un pendu déjà mur,
Et chacun jusque'aux yeux plantait son bec impur
Dans tous les coins saignants de cette pourriture.

Les yeux étaient deux trous, et du ventre effondré
Les intestins pesants lui coulaient sur les cuisses,
35   L'organe de l'amour avait fait leurs délices,
Et ces bourreaux l'avaient cruellement châtré.

Sous les pieds un troupeau de jaloux quadrupèdes
Le museau relevé tournoyaient et rôdait;
Une plus grande bête au milieu s'agitait,
40   Comme un exécuteur entouré de ses aides.

Habitant de Cythère, enfant d'un ciel si beau,
Silencieusement tu souffrais ces insultes
En expiation de tes anciens cultes
Et des péchés qui t'ont interdit le tombeau.

45   Pauvre pendu muet, tes douleurs sont les miennes.
Je sentis à l'aspect de tes membres flottants,
Comme un vomissement remonter vers mes dents
Le long fleuve de fiel de mes douleurs anciennes;

Devant toi, pauvre diable au souvenir si cher,
50   J'ai senti tous les becs et toutes les mâchoires
Des corbeaux lancinants et des panthères noires
Qui jadis aimaient tant à triturer ma chair.

Le ciel etait charmant, la mer était unie.
Pour moi, tout était noir et sanglant désormais,
55 Hélas! et j'avais comme en un suaire épais
Le coeur enseveli dans cette allégorie.

Dans ton île, ô Vénus, je n'ai trouvé debout
Qu'un gibet dégoûtant où pendait mon image.
Oh Seigneur! donnez-moi la force et le courage
60 De contempler mon coeur et mon corps sans dégout.

Notes

Preface

1. Benjamin's essays on Baudelaire have been published in one volume under the title *Charles Baudelaire: A Lyric Poet in the Era of High Capitalism*, trans. Harry Zohn (London: NLB, 1973).

2. (Berkeley: University of California Press, 1977), 1–2. Further references to the book will be given parenthetically in the text.

3. Such exception was taken by Jonathan Culler in his review of the book: "The idea that by predicating a series of metaphors of the beloved a poet could escape the "vorace ironie" of self-consciousness, could escape from the self, is one which would have amused Baudelaire, who was not unfamiliar with irony and tropes. Poems which address the problem of figurative language, such as 'Obsession' and 'Alchimie de la douleur,' make it clear that the production of images or metaphors does not lead to an escape from self but rather entraps one in a universe of one's own vision, and the love poems give one no good reason for believing that matters change substantially when metaphors are applied to a woman" (*Comparative Literature* 31 [Spring, 1979], 177).

4. (Paris: Flammarion, 1979), 10. Further references to the book will given parenthetically in the text.

5. *Oeuvres complètes*, ed. Claude Pichois (Paris: Gallimard, 1975), I, 27. All further citations of Baudelaire's poems and essays will come from this edition, hereafter abbreviated *O.C.*, I or II, unless otherwise noted. All citations from Baudelaire's letters will be drawn from the volumes of the *Correspondance générale* (hereafter abbreviated *C.G.*) in the *Oeuvres complètes de Charles Baudelaire*, ed. Jacques Crépet (Paris: Conard, 1947), *Correspondance* series.

Chapter 1. Le Point de Départ

1. These are the words of Stadler, with whom Nerval stayed during part of this time. Cited by Jean Richer, ed., *Oeuvres de Gérard de Nerval* (Paris: Gallimard, 1960), I, xxvii.

2. Letter of March 5, 1852 (*C.G.*, I, 157).

3. Letter of March 20, 1852 (ibid., 155–56).

4. In *Mon coeur mis à nu* Baudelaire writes: "Ma fureur au coup d'état.

Combien j'ai essuyé de coups de fusil. Encore un Bonaparte! quelle honte!" (*O.C.*, I, 679).

5. Letter of March 27, 1852 (*C.G.*, I, 163).

6. Prarond writes, in his introduction to *Quelques poètes nouveaux* (1852): "Amongst others whom we hope not to have lost forever, there is one particularly, who enjoyed the strange fate of having made a name for himself without publishing a single line of verse, merely by reciting the noblest poetry to a small gathering of friends. This poet . . . is Monsieur Baudelaire. We sincerely hope that, having become a poet once more, and remaining one, he may occupy the attention of the critic who next undertakes what I am attempting today." Cited in Enid Starkie, *Baudelaire* (New York: New Directions, 1958), 220.

7. Undated letter (*C.G.*, I, 153).

8. Maxime Du Camp, in his *Souvenirs littéraires*, attributes this remark to Gautier. Cited in Starkie, *Baudelaire*, 221.

9. See Starkie, *Baudelaire*, 198–99, for a discussion of the several possible dates of composition.

10. See, for example, the letter to Théophile Thoré, January 20, 1864 (*C.G.*, III).

11. It might be argued that Baudelaire "means" only "gaudy" or "shocking" when he writes *voyant*, since he uses the word in clearly that sense in other letters about his poems. Writing to Poulet-Malassis in 1856 with regard to the arrangement of the poems in *Les Fleurs du Mal*, he states: "Il nous faut faire un volume composé seulement de bonnes choses: peu de matière qui paraisse beaucoup, et qui soit tres voyante" (*C.G.*, I, 408). The clearer context in this case does not necessarily rule out the possibility of an intentional wordplay in the note to Gautier. Moreover, it cannot preclude an investigation of the metonymic path between the writing of the word *voyante* and the mention of the *Voyage à Cythère*.

12. *Oeuvres de Gérard de Nerval*, ed. Albert Béguin and Jean Richer (Paris: Gallimard, 1961), II, 61. Further page references will be given parenthetically in the text.

13. See the appendix for a complete reproduction of the text of 1852, based on Pichois' list of *variantes* in *O.C.*, I, 1071–73.

14. It is a commonplace to read the poem as motivated by Baudelaire's syphilitic condition. The acrimony to which I refer is apparent in Antoine Adam's response to this biographical reductionism in the notes to his edition of *Les Fleurs du Mal* (Paris: Garnier Frères, 1961): "On admirera les exégètes qui découvrent ici une allusion de Baudelaire à l'impuissance sexuelle qu'ils ont la bonté du lui attribuer" (416–17).

15. *The Limits of Symbolism: Studies of Five Modern French Poets* (Chicago: University of Chicago Press, 1966), 83.

16. There remains, and will luckily always remain, more to be said at every step of my argument. In the case of this strange prayer, for instance, we ought to remember that Claudel was moved by it, seeing it as the single glimmer of light amidst all the smoke and darkness that filled the imagination of "poor Baudelaire." Or we might consider at greater length how prayer can function rhetorically in a manner similar to that of apostrophe and prosopopeia, constituting a speaking subject over against a "you" that is an effect of language. Such a discussion would have to call upon Gregory Bateson, "The Cybernetics of 'Self': A Theory of Alcoholism," in *Steps to an Ecology of Mind* (New York: Random House, 1972), 309–37; Jonathan Culler, "Apostrophe," in *The Pursuit of Signs*, 135–54; and Paul de Man, "Hypogram and Inscription: Michael Riffaterre's Poetics of Reading," *Diacritics* 11 (Winter, 1981), 17–35. Finally, I refer the reader seeking a comprehensive thematic reading of the poem to Weinberg's in *The Limits of Symbolism*.

17. Trans. James Strachey (New York: Norton, 1961), 11–20.

18. *The Limits of Symbolism*, 69.

19. For a recent discussion of syphilis in connection with a host of literary motifs, see Patrick Wald Lasowski, *Syphilis, Essai sur la littérature française du XIXe siècle* (Paris: Gallimard, 1982). One can only regret that this study does not include a theory of "syphilitic" language, nor propose a systematic poetics of syphilis.

20. These are the problematics of the subject that Hegel calls the "unhappy consciousness," and the discussion of them in relation to "Romantic irony" and autobiographical writing has become ubiquitous. The most powerful enunciation of the problem remains Jacques Lacan's essay "The Mirror Stage," in *Ecrits*, trans. Alan Sheridan (New York: Norton, 1977), 1–7. The most graceful application of Lacan's lesson in exploring the relations among subject, image, and language is to be found throughout *Roland Barthes par Roland Barthes* (Paris: Seuil, 1975).

21. See Freud to Rolland, July 14, July 20, 1929, January 19, 1930, and May, 1931, in *Letters of Sigmund Freud, 1873–1939*, ed. Ernst L. Freud, trans. Tania and James Stern (London: Hogarth Press, 1970).

22. *O.C.*, II, 44–49.

23. Pantagruel tells the story of the announcement of the death of Pan in chapter 28 of the fourth book. His gloss of it follows the evangelical tradition: "C'est le bon Pan, le grand pasteur, qui, comme atteste le bergier passionné Corydon, non seulement a en amour et affection ses brebis, mais

aussi ses bergiers. A la mort duquel feurent plaincts, souspirs, affroys et lamentations en toute la machine de l'Univers, cieulx, terre, mer, enfers. A ceste miene interpretation compete le temps, car cestuy tresbon, tresgrand Pan, nostre unique Servateur, mourut lez Hierusalem, regnant en Rome Tibere Caesar" (*Le Quart Livre*, ed. Robert Marichal [Geneva: Droz, 1947], 138).

24. *Les Fleurs de Mal*, ed. Adam, 416.

25. *Baudelaire*, 198.

26. *Mercure de France*, October 15, 1925. Cited by Léon Cellier, *Baudelaire et Hugo* (Paris: Corti, 1970), 70.

27. F. Strowski, *Comoedia*, May 9, 1923. Cited in *Baudelaire et Hugo*, 71.

28. *Baudelaire et Hugo*, 76.

29. Trans. John Macquarrie and Edward Robinson (New York: Harper and Row, 1962), 231.

30. *The Limits of Symbolism*, 66.

31. Ibid., 66–67; my italics.

32. *O.C.*, I, 117–19. Further citations of the poem will be drawn from this edition, with line numbers given where needed for clarity.

33. *O.C.*, I, 664–65. Cellier finds 1855 to be the probable date of composition for these lines (*Baudelaire et Hugo*, 67).

34. In Freud's "Analysis of a Phobia in a Five-year-old Boy," the child, Hans, comes to identify the condition of animacy with the possession of a penis. Freud writes: "There can be no doubt as to the existence of Hans' sexual curiosity; but it roused the spirit of inquiry in him and enabled him to arrive at genuine abstract knowledge.

"When he was at the station once (at three and three-quarters) he saw some water being let out of an engine. 'Oh look,' he said, 'the engine's widdling. Where's it got its widdler?' After a little he added in reflective tones: 'A dog and a horse have widdlers; a table and a chair haven't.' He had thus got hold of an essential characteristic for differentiating between animate and inanimate objects." (*The Sexual Enlightenment of Children* [New York: Collier, 1963], 51, 53n10).

It is the identification of life with the attribute of a penis that leads the boy to "see" a small "widdler" on the body of his infant sister. His abstract thinking is rooted in a binary logic that in turn reflects the rigidity of the gender roles in his world.

35. In a reading like Weinberg's explication, where the assumption of a unified voice underlies the poem's structural unity, the deixis must be maintained as pointing at the object of identification, so as not to contaminate the process of identification in which the allegorizing voice of the poem is engaged. Thus we find him insisting that "'allégorie' is not to be

taken in any technical literary sense" (*The Limits of Symbolism*, 85). This seems a strange stricture to impose on a rather technical and literary poet.

36. In equally ominous terms, Lacan ends "The Mirror Stage" as follows: "We can thus understand the inertia characteristic of the formations of the I, and find there the most extensive definition of neurosis—just as the captation of the subject by the situation gives us the most general formula for madness, not only the madness that lies behind the walls of asylums, but also the madness that deafens the world with its sound and fury."

Chapter 2. The Interference of Laughter

1. *O.C.*, II, 538–39.

2. For a discussion of *Le Thyrse* as a meditation on metaphoricity, see Richard Klein, "Straight Lines and Arabesques: Metaphor of Metaphor," *Yale French Studies* 45 (1970), 64–86.

3. *Pensées sur la religion et sur quelques autres sujets*, ed. Louis Lafuma (Paris: Editions du Luxembourg, 1951), 42.

4. Trans. J. H. Bernard (New York: Hafner, 1951), 149; translation modified.

5. The most pertinent readings of the *Critique of Judgment* are the complementary studies by Jacques Derrida: "Economimésis," in *Mimésis des articulations* (Paris: Aubier-Flammarion, 1975), and "Parergon," in *La Vérité en peinture* (Paris: Flammarion, 1978).

6. Section 44, pp. 147–49.

7. (Paris: Larousse, 1972), 77.

8. Trans. James Strachey (New York: Norton, 1963), 96.

9. Pp. 97–102.

10. In a letter to Fernand Desnoyers that was to serve as an epigraph to the two *Crépuscules* in a small volume of verse, Baudelaire writes: "Je ne croirai jamais que l'âme des Dieux habite dans les plantes, et quand même elle y habiterait, je m'en soucierais médiocrement, et considererais la mienne comme du'un bien plus haut prix que celle des légumes sanctifiés" (*C.G.*, I, 322).

11. Hernani's exclamation occurs in the fourth scene of Act III, as part of a definition of unicity:

> Tu me crois, peut-être,
> Un homme comme sont tous les autres, un être
> Intelligent, qui court droit au but qu'il rêva.
> Détrompe-toi. Je suis une force qui va!

Agent aveugle et sourd de mystères funèbres!
Une âme de malheur faite avec des ténèbres!
Ou vais-je? je ne sais. . . .

(80, ll. 989–95)

The character has become the personification of "genius," whose creative force entails a certain blindness.

12. To quote from *The Language of Psychoanalysis:* "Experiences, impressions and memory traces may be revised at a later date to fit in with fresh experiences or with the attainment of a new stage of development. They may in that event be endowed not only with a new meaning but also with psychical effectiveness" (J. Laplanche and J. B. Pontalis, trans. Donald Nicholson-Smith [New York: Norton, 1973], 111). A fine explanation of the implications of this complex temporality of meaning can be found in Cynthia Chase's article "Oedipal Textuality: Reading Freud's Reading of Oedipus," *Diacritics* 9 (Spring, 1979), 54–71.

13. See John Brenkman, "The Other and the One: Psychoanalysis, Reading, The Symposium," *Yale French Studies* 55/56 (1977), for a lucid discussion of the notion of the Other in Lacan, a term that functions "to account for three interrelated scenes of communications in which the subject is determined by the signifier: normative linguistic exchange, the dream, and the infant's relation to the mother" (437).

14. *La Révolution du langage poétique* (Paris: Seuil, 1974), 45; my translation.

15. "Sexuality: A Fact of Discourse," in *Homosexualities and French Literature,* ed. George Stambolian and Elaine Marks (Ithaca: Cornell University Press, 1979), 45.

16. *La Révolution du langage poétique,* 45–46.

17. It is worth noting that Baudelaire's discussion of psychological affects is qualified by the esthetic concept of the *je-ne-sais-quoi.* A page earlier, speaking of the *Sage* who hesitates before laughing, he likewise refers to "je ne sais quel malaise et quelle inquiétude." An esthetic mode and a psychological state begin clearly to overlap.

18. *Beyond the Pleasure Principle,* trans. James Strachey (New York: Norton, 1961), p. 6. See also Heidegger's distinction between anxiety and fear in paragraph 40 of *Being and Time:* "The Basic State-of-Mind of Anxiety as a Distinctive Way in which Dasein is Disclosed," 228–35.

19. *The Problem of Anxiety,* trans. Henry Alden Bunker (New York: Norton, 1936), 73. My reading of Freud's essay is deeply indebted to an unpublished article by Richard Klein, "Oxymorons of Anxiety, or the Influence of Baba Ram Dass on Harold Bloom."

20. The laughter of others isolates the one who is not able to join in the laughter. For Sartre, laughter's chief function is to consolidate individuals in a series by scapegoating one who has broken a code of propriety. See his analysis of laughter in *L'Idiot de la famille: Gustave Flaubert de 1821 à 1857* (Paris: Gallimard, 1971), I, 811–24.

21. *Being and Time*, 233.

22. *Pensées*, 46–47.

23. "Qu'est-ce que l'art? Prostitution," *Fusées*, *O.C.*, I, 649.

24. "L'Irrémédiable," *O.C.*, I, 79.

25. *O.C.*, I, 23–24.

26. "L'échec de Baudelaire," in *La Part du feu* (Paris: Gallimard, 1949), 133–51.

27. *O.C.*, II, 678.

28. In entry 84, "On the Origin of Poetry," of *The Gay Science*, trans. Walter Kaufmann (New York: Random House, 1974), Nietzsche writes: "Rhythm is a compulsion; it engenders an unconquerable urge to yield and join in; not only our feet follow the beat but the soul does, too—probably, one surmised, the soul of the gods as well! Thus one tried to *compel* the gods by using rhythm and to force their hand; poetry was thrown at them like a magical snare" (139). The poet of *The Gay Science* is engaged in shifting the optic by which one traditionally either aligned or disjoined Poetry and Truth; the poet of Le Masque would have been sympathetic to such a project.

29. J.-D. Hubert, *L'Esthétique des "Fleurs du Mal"* (Geneva: Pierre Cailler, 1953), 231.

30. The *clinamen* is the first of Harold Bloom's six "revisionary ratios" by which a younger poet, or ephebe, counters the work of a precursor. In *The Anxiety of Influence* (New York: Oxford University Press, 1973), Bloom defines the clinamen as: "poetic misreading or misprision proper; I take the word from Lucretius, where it means a 'swerve' of the atoms so as to make change possible in the universe. A poet swerved away from his precursor, by so reading his precursor's poem as to execute a clinamen in relation to it. This appears as a corrective movement in his own poem, which implies that the precursor's poem went accurately up to a certain point, but then should have swerved, precisely in the direction that the new poem moves" (14). The turning of allegory round itself in the process of revising the "Voyage à Cythère" constitutes a radical "swerve," or clinamen. Some of the implications of a "poetic misreading" of oneself will be discussed in the following chapter.

Chapter 3. Without-Within

1. "Anthropomorphism and Trope in the Lyric," in *The Rhetoric of Romanticism* (New York: Columbia University Press, 1984), 262.

2. Mallarmé's prose and letters are replete with remarks that try to typify the way in which the poet sets words to working so as to distinguish them from the words of everyday. The cited remark was chosen for its imperialist resonance, aligning it with the note by Baudelaire. Other, more radical notations about poetic language could have been cited, but my point here is to suggest how the metaphorics of an imperialist culture come to invade the articulation of poetic programs.

3. "Fetishism," in *Sexuality and the Psychology of Love* (New York: Macmillan, 1963), 216.

4. "From Imagination to Immediacy in French Poetry," *The Romantic Review* 39 (February 1948), 34.

5. "The Originality of Baudelaire's 'Le Cygne'," in Ernest Beaumont et al., eds., *Order and Adventure in Post-Romantic French Poetry* (Oxford: Blackwell, 1973), 38.

6. *The Pursuit of Signs* (Ithaca: Cornell University Press, 1981), 144.

7. "The Danaïdes' Vessel: On Reading Baudelaire's Allegories," in Robert L. Mitchell, ed., *Pre-text/Text/Context* (Columbus: Ohio State University Press, 1980), 141.

8. "Marx's Relevance for Second Empire Literature: Baudelaire's *Le Cygne*," unpublished paper cited by Ross Chambers, "Du Temps des 'Chats' au temps du 'Cygne'," *Oeuvres et critiques* 9, no. 2 (1984).

9. On the interchangeability of these terms in Baudelaire's lexicon, see F. W. Leakey, *Baudelaire and Nature* (New York: Barnes and Noble, 1969), 225; Lloyd James Austin, *L'Univers poétique de Baudelaire* (Paris: Mercure de France, 1956), 162–70; and Margaret Gilman, *The Idea of Poetry in France* (Cambridge: Harvard University Press, 1958), 258–59.

10. Editors date the text, based on Prarond's claim of having heard at least the first two lines recited, from before the end of 1843.

11. (Paris: Colin, 1955), 181–82.

12. I follow Leakey, *Baudelaire and Nature*, 236, in his reading of "spirituel" in Baudelaire as equivalent to "moral" or "mental."

13. In *Poétique 3* (1970), 339. Other references to Deguy's article will be given in parentheses.

14. On the concept of the hymen as the double action of veiling and proximity, see Jacques Derrida's reading of Mallarmé, "La Double Séance," in *La Dissemination* (Paris: Seuil, 1972), 199–317.

15. Letter to Alphonse Toussenel, cited by Pichois, *O.C.*, II, 1141.

16. Victor Cousin was the primary importer and interpreter of German philosophy for Baudelaire's generation. His "eclectic" philosophy and courses on aesthetics led to what Baudelaire calls, in his article on Gautier, "La fameuse doctrine de l'indissolubilité du Beau, du Vrai et du Bien" (O.C., II, 111). On the influence of Cousin's adaptation of German philosophy on the history of French poetry, see L. J. Austin, L'Univers poétique de Baudelaire, 139–84.

17. Critique of Judgment, trans. J. H. Bernard (New York: Macmillan, 1951), 32. Other references to this work will be given parenthetically in the text.

18. For an analysis of this strange circuit of self-giving, and a definition of what is at stake in it, see Jacques Derrida, "Economimésis," in Mimésis des articulations, ed. Sylviane Agacinski et al. (Paris: Flammarion, 1975).

Epilogue

1. Charles Baudelaire: A Lyric Poet in the Era of High Capitalism, trans. Harry Zohn (London: NLB, 1973), 68. Benjamin's discussion of Le Soleil begins his analysis of Baudelaire's "modernism," which he interprets as resulting from the disappearance of the ritual (kultische) from human experience, and its replacement by the novelty of the "shock."

Bibliography

Austin, Lloyd James. *L'Univers poétique de Baudelaire: symbolisme et symbolique*. Paris: Mercure de France, 1956.

Barthes, Roland. *Roland Barthes sur Roland Barthes*. Paris: Seuil, 1975.

Bataille, Georges. *La Littérature et le mal*. Paris: Gallimard, 1957.

Baudelaire, Charles. *Correspondance générale*. 4 vols. of *Oeuvres complètes*. Edited by Jacques Crépet. Paris: Conard, 1947.

——. *Les Fleurs du Mal*. Edited by Antoine Adam. Paris: Garnier Frères, 1961.

——. *Les Fleurs du Mal*. Edited by Adrien van Bever. Paris: Crès, 1925.

——. *Les Fleurs du Mal*. Edited by Jacques Crépet and Georges Blin. Paris: Corti, 1942.

——. *Oeuvres complètes*. 2 vols. Edited by Claude Pichois. Paris: Gallimard, 1975.

Benjamin, Walter. *Charles Baudelaire: A Lyric Poet in the Era of High Capitalism*. Translated by Harry Zohn. London: New Left Books, 1973.

Bersani, Leo. *Baudelaire and Freud*. Berkeley: University of California Press, 1977.

Blanchot, Maurice. *La Part du feu*. Paris: Gallimard, 1949.

Blin, Georges. *Baudelaire*. Paris: Gallimard, 1939.

——. *Le Sadisme de Baudelaire*. Paris: Corti, 1948.

Bloom, Harold. *The Anxiety of Influence*. New York: Oxford University Press, 1973.

Brenkman, John. "The Other and the One: Psychoanalysis, Reading, the Symposium." *Yale French Studies* 55/56 (1977), 397–456.

Butor, Michel. *Histoire extraordinaire*. Translated by Richard Howard. London: Jonathan Cape, 1969.

Cassagne, Albert. *Versification et métrique de Ch. Baudelaire*. Paris: Hachette, 1906.

Cellier, Léon. *Baudelaire et Hugo*. Paris: Corti, 1970.

Chase, Cynthia. "Oedipal Textuality: Reading Freud's Reading of Oedipus." *Diacritics* 9, no. 1 (1979), 54–71.

Chérix, Robert-Benoit. *Commentaire des 'Fleurs du Mal'*. Geneva: Pierre Cailler, 1949.

Clark, Timothy J. *The Absolute Bourgeois: Artists and Politics in France, 1848–1851*. Greenwich, Conn.: New York Graphic Society Ltd., 1973.

Culler, Jonathan. *The Pursuit of Signs*. Ithaca, N.Y.: Cornell University Press, 1981.

Deguy, Michel. "Le Corps de Jeanne." *Poétique* 3 (1970), 334–47.

—. "L'Esthétique de Baudelaire." *Critique* 23 (1967), 695–717.

Deleuze, Gilles. *Présentation de Sacher-Masoch: le froid et le cruel.* Paris: Minuit, 1967.

De Man, Paul. *Blindness and Insight.* New York: Oxford University Press, 1971.

—. "Hypogram and Inscription: Michael Riffaterre's Poetics of Reading." *Diacritics* 11, no. 4 (1981), 17–35.

—. "The Rhetoric of Temporality." In *Interpretation: Theory and Practice,* edited by Charles S. Singleton, 173–209. Baltimore: Johns Hopkins University Press, 1969.

Derrida, Jacques. *La Dissemination.* Paris: Seuil, 1972.

—. "Economimésis." In *Mimésis des articulations,* edited by Sylviane Agacinski et al. Paris: Flammarion, 1975.

—. *La Vérité en peinture.* Paris: Flammarion, 1978.

Fletcher, Angus. *Allegory, the Theory of a Symbolic Mode.* Ithaca, N.Y.: Cornell University Press, 1964.

Fondane, Benjamin. *Baudelaire et l'expérience du gouffre.* Paris: Seghers, 1972.

Freud, Ernst L., ed. *Letters of Sigmund Freud, 1873–1939.* Translated by Tania and James Stern. London: Hogarth Press, 1970.

Freud, Sigmund. *Beyond the Pleasure Principle.* Translated by James Strachey. New York: Norton, 1961.

—. *Civilisation and Its Discontents.* Translated by James Strachey. New York: Norton, 1961.

—. *Jokes and Their Relation to the Unconscious.* Translated by James Strachey. New York: Norton, 1963.

—. *The Problem of Anxiety.* Translated by Henry Alden Bunker. New York: Norton, 1936.

—. *The Sexual Enlightenment of Children.* Edited by Philip Rieff. New York: Macmillan, 1963.

—. *Sexuality and the Psychology of Love.* Edited by Philip Rieff. New York: Macmillan, 1963.

Gilman, Margaret. "From Imagination to Immediacy in French Poetry." *The Romantic Review* 39, no. 1 (1948), 30–49.

—. *The Idea of Poetry in France.* Cambridge: Harvard University Press, 1958.

Heidegger, Martin. *Being and Time.* Translated by John Macquarrie and Edward Robinson. New York: Harper and Row, 1962.

—. *Poetry, Language, Thought.* Translated by Albert Hofstadter. New York: Harper and Row, 1971.

Hubert, J.-D. *L'Esthétique des 'Fleurs du Mal'.* Geneva: Pierre Cailler, 1953.

Hugo, Victor. *Poésie.* Vol. I. Edited by Bernard Levilliot. Paris: Seuil, 1972.

—. *Préface de Cromwell.* Paris: Larousse, 1972.

Johnson, Barbara. *Défigurations du langage poétique: la seconde révolution baudelairienne.* Paris: Flammarion, 1979.

Kant, Emmanuel. *The Critique of Judgment.* Translated by J. H. Bernard. New York: Hafner, 1951.

Klein, Richard. "Kant's Sunshine." *Diacritics* 11, no. 2 (1981), 26–41.

—. "Thyrsus: The Ironic Stance of Baudelaire's Poetry." Ph.D. dissertation, Yale University, 1968.

Kristeva, Julia. *La Révolution du langage poétique.* Paris: Seuil, 1974.

Labrunie, Gérard. *Oeuvres de Gérard de Nerval.* 2 vols. Edited by Albert Béguin and Jean Richer. Paris: Gallimard, 1960.

Lacan, Jacques. *Ecrits.* Translated by Alan Sheridan. New York: Norton, 1977.

—. *The Language of the Self: The Function of Language in Psychoanalysis.* Translated by Anthony Wilden. Baltimore: Johns Hopkins University Press, 1968.

Laplanche, Jean. *Life and Death in Psychoanalysis.* Translated by Jeffrey Mehlman. Baltimore: Johns Hopkins University Press, 1976.

Lasowski, Patrick Wald. *Syphilis: essai sur la littérature française du XIXᵉ siècle.* Paris: Gallimard, 1982.

Leakey, F. W. *Baudelaire and Nature.* New York: Barnes and Noble, 1969.

Leclaire, Serge. "Sexuality: A Fact of Discourse." In *Homosexualities and French Literature,* edited by George Stambolian and Elaine Marks. Ithaca, N.Y.: Cornell University Press, 1979.

Mouquet, Jules, and W. T. Bandy *Baudelaire en 1848: La Tribune Nationale.* Paris: Emile-Paul Frères, 1946.

Pascal, Blaise. *Pensées sur la religion et sur quelques autres sujets.* Edited by Louis Lafuma. Paris: Editions du Luxembourg, 1951.

Richard, Jean-Pierre. *Poésie et profondeur.* Paris: Seuil, 1955.

Ruff, Marcel. *L'Esprit du mal et l'esthétique baudelairienne.* Paris: Colin, 1955.

Sartre, Jean-Paul. *Baudelaire.* Paris: Gallimard, 1963.

Starkie, Enid. *Baudelaire.* New York: New Directions, 1958.

Weinberg, Bernard. *The Limits of Symbolism.* Chicago: University of Chicago Press, 1966.

Wittgenstein, Ludwig. *Tractatus Logico-Philosophicus.* Translated by C. K. Ogden. London: Routledge and Kegan Paul, Ltd., 1922.

Wohlfarth, Irving. "Perte d'Auréole: The Emergence of the Dandy." *MLN* 84, no. 4 (1970), 529–71.

Index